DICTION COACH
ARIAS FOR
BARITONE

International Phonetic Alphabet and Diction Lessons
Recorded by a Professional, Native Speaker Coach

Diction Recordings

Corradina Caporello, Italian
Kathryn LaBouff, English
Irene Spiegelman, German
Pierre Vallet, French

International Phonetic Alphabet

Martha Gerhart, Italian and French
Kathryn LaBouff, English
Irene Spiegelman, German

This Diction Coach includes all arias from *Arias for Baritone* (HL50481100).
For plot notes and line-by-line translations, please see the original aria collection.

ED 4406

On the cover: "L'opéra de Paris" by Raoul Dufy
Used by permission of The Phillips Collection, Washington D.C.

ISBN 978-1-4234-1311-0

www.schirmer.com
www.halleonard.com

G. SCHIRMER, *Inc.*

DISTRIBUTED BY

HAL•LEONARD®
CORPORATION
7777 W. BLUEMOUND RD. P.O. BOX 13819 MILWAUKEE, WI 53213

PREFACE

What a wonderful opportunity for singers these volumes represent. The diction coaches recorded on the companion CDs are from the staffs of the Metropolitan Opera and The Julliard School, whose specialty is working with singers. I personally have had the opportunity to study Italian with Ms. Caporello and have experienced the sheer delight of learning operatic texts with a linguist who is devoted to the art of singing.

There are two versions of the text recorded for each aria.

1. Recitation

The Coach speaks the text of the aria as an actor would speak it, using spoken diction and capturing the mood. The guttural "R" is pronounced as in speech in French and German. Even in these free recitations, these experienced coaches are obviously informed as to how the text relates to the musical setting.

2. Diction Lessons

Dividing the text of the aria into short phrases, the coach speaks a line at a time very slowly and deliberately, without interpretation, making each word sound distinct. Time is allowed for the repetition of each phrase. In this slow version the French and German coaches adapt the guttural "R" in a manner appropriate for opera singers. The coaches in all languages make small adjustments recommended for singers in these slowly enunciated diction lessons, including elisions and liaisons between word sounds as related to the sung phrase.

There is not one universally used approach to International Phonetic Alphabet. The article before each language should be studied carefully for comprehension of the specific approach to IPA for each language in this edition.

The diction recordings can be used in many ways but a highly recommended plan is this. After carefully working regularly with the recorded diction lesson and the related IPA over several days, one should be able to reach fluency in the aria text. As an exercise separate from singing the aria, the singer should then speak the text freely, as in the diction coach's recitation. The singer likely will be inspired by the recitations recorded by the diction coaches, but after pronunciation is mastered might even begin to discover informed and individual interpretations in reciting the aria text.

By paying attention to the libretto of an aria, or an entire role, apart from the music, the opera singer can begin to understand character and interpretation in a way that would not be possible if the text is only considered by singing it. Just as an actor explores a script and a character from various historical, intellectual and emotional angles, so must the opera singer. Understanding the stated and unstated meanings of the text is fundamental in becoming a convincing actor on the opera stage, or on the opera audition stage. But the opera singer is only half done. After a thorough exploration of the words, one must discover how the composer interpreted the text and how best to express that interpretation. In great music for the opera stage, that exploration can be a fascinating lifetime journey.

Robert L. Larsen
June, 2008

CONTENTS

CD TRACK LIST
DISC ONE

CD TRACK LIST
DISC TWO

		Recitation	Diction Lesson
Arias in French			
31	About French IPA		
	CARMEN		
33	Votre toast, je peux vous le rendre	1	2
	FAUST		
35	Avant de quitter ces lieux	3	4
	HAMLET		
37	Ô vin, dissipe la trestesse	5	6
	HÉRODIADE		
38	Vision fugitive	7	8
	ROMÉO ET JULIETTE		
40	Mab, la reine des mensonges	9	10
	THAÏS		
43	Voilà donc la terrible cité	11	12
Arias in German			
45	About German IPA		
	HÄNSEL UND GRETEL		
48	Ach, wir armen Leute	13	14
	TANNHÄUSER		
49	O! du mein holder Abendstern	15	16
	DIE ZAUBERFLÖTE		
51	Der Vogelfänger bin ich ja	17	18
52	Ein Mädchen oder Weibchen	19	20
Arias in English			
54	About English IPA		
	THE BALLAD OF BABY DOE		
57	Warm as the autumn light	21	22
	VANESSA		
59	You rascal you! I never knew you had a soul	23	24

ABOUT THE ITALIAN IPA TRANSLITERATIONS
by Martha Gerhart

While the IPA is currently the diction learning tool of choice for singers not familiar with the foreign languages in which they sing, differences in transliterations exist in diction manuals and on the internet, just as differences of pronunciation exist in the Italian language itself.

The Italian transliterations in this volume reflect the following choices:

All unstressed "e's" and "o's" are *closed*. This choice is based on the highest form of the spoken language, as in the authoritative Italian dictionary edited by Zingarelli. However, in practice, singers may well make individual choices as to *closed* or *open* depending upon the vocal tessitura and technical priorities.

Also, there are many Italian words (such as "sento," "cielo," and etc.) for which, in practice, both *closed* and *open* vowels in the *stressed* syllable are perfectly acceptable.

The "nasal 'm'" symbol [ɱ], indicating that the letter "n" assimilates before a "v" or an "f" (such as "inferno" becoming [im ˈfɛr no] in execution, is not used in these transliterations. This choice was a practical one to avoid confusion on the part of the student who might wonder why "in" is transcribed as if it were "im," unlike in any dictionary. However, students are encouraged to use the [ɱ] as advised by experts.

Double consonants which result, in execution, from *phrasal doubling* (*raddoppiamento sintattico*) are not transliterated as such; but students should utilize this sophistication of Italian lyric diction as appropriate.

The syllabic divisions in these transliterations are in the interest of encouraging the singer to lengthen the vowel before a single consonant rather than making an incorrect double consonant, and also to encourage the singer, when there are two consonants, the first of which is *l, m, n*, or *r*, to give more strength to the first of those two consonants.

Intervocalic "s's" are transliterated as *voiced*, despite the fact that in many words ("casa," "così," etc.) the "s" is *unvoiced* in the language (and in the above-mentioned dictionary). Preferred practice for singers is to *voice* those "s's" in the interest of legato; yet, an unvoiced "s" pronunciation in those cases is not incorrect. (*Note*: words which combine a prefix and a stem beginning with an unvoiced "s" ["risolvi," "risanare," etc.] retain the unvoiced "s" of the prefix in singing as well as in speech.)

Many Italian words have alternate pronunciations given in the best dictionaries, particularly regarding closed or open vowels. In my IPA transliterations I chose the first given pronunciation, which is not always the preferred pronunciation in common Italian usage as spoken by Corradina Caporello on the accompanying CDs. I defer to my respected colleague in all cases for her expert pronunciation of beautiful Italian diction.

Pronunciation Key

IPA Symbol	Approximate sound in English	IPA Symbol	Approximate sound in English
[i]	f<u>ee</u>t	[s]	<u>s</u>et
[e]	pot<u>a</u>to	[z]	<u>z</u>ip
[ɛ]	b<u>e</u>d	[l]	<u>l</u>ip
[a]	f<u>a</u>ther	[ʎ]	mil<u>li</u>on
[ɔ]	t<u>au</u>t		
[o]	t<u>o</u>te	[ɾ]	as *British* "ve<u>r</u>y" – flipped "r"
[u]	t<u>u</u>be	[r]	no English equivalent – rolled "r"
[j]	<u>Y</u>ale		
[w]	<u>w</u>atch	[n]	<u>n</u>ame
		[m]	<u>m</u>op
[b]	<u>b</u>eg	[ŋ]	a<u>n</u>chor
[p]	<u>p</u>et	[ɲ]	o<u>ni</u>on
[d]	<u>d</u>eep	[tʃ]	<u>ch</u>eese
[t]	<u>t</u>op	[dʒ]	<u>G</u>eorge
[g]	<u>G</u>ordon	[dz]	fee<u>ds</u>
[k]	<u>k</u>it	[ts]	fi<u>ts</u>
[v]	<u>v</u>et		
[f]	<u>f</u>it	[ː]	indicates doubled consonants
[ʃ]	<u>sh</u>e	[ˈ]	indicates the primary stress; the syllable following the mark is stressed

IL BARBIERE DI SIVIGLIA

music: Gioachino Rossini
libretto: Cesare Sterbini (after *Le Barbier de Séville*, a comedy by Pierre Augustin Caron de Beaumarchais)

Largo al factotum

la	ran	la	ˈle ɾa	la	ran	la	la
La	**ran**	**la**	**lera,**	**la**	**ran**	**la**	**la...**
la	*tra*	*la*	*la*	*la*	*tra*	*la*	*la*

ˈlar go	al	fak ˈtɔ tum	ˈdel: la	tʃit: ˈta
Largo	**al**	**factotum**	**della**	**città,**
make way	*for the*	*factotum*	*of the*	*city*

ˈprɛ sto	a	bot: ˈte ga
Presto	**a**	**bottega,**
quick	*to*	*[the] shop*

ke	ˈlal ba	ɛ	dʒa
chè	**l'alba**	**è**	**già,**
because	*the dawn*	*it is*	*already*

a	ke	bɛl	ˈvi ve ɾe
Ah	**che**	**bel**	**vivere,**
ah	*what*	*beautiful*	*living*

ke	bɛl	pja ˈtʃe ɾe
che	**bel**	**piacere**
what	*beautiful*	*pleasure*

per	un	bar ˈbjɛ ɾe	di	kwa li ˈta
per	**un**	**barbiere**	**di**	**qualità!**
for	*a*	*barber*	*of*	*quality*

a	ˈbra vo	ˈfi ga ɾo	bra ˈvis: si mo
Ah	**bravo,**	**Figaro,**	**bravissimo!**
ah	*well done*	*Figaro*	*very well done*

for tu na ˈtis: si mo	per	ve ɾi ˈta
Fortunatissimo	**per**	**verità!**
very lucky	*in*	*truth*

ˈbra vo
Bravo!
well done

ˈpron to	a	far	ˈtut: to
Pronto	**a**	**far**	**tutto,**
ready	*to*	*[to] do*	*everything*

la	ˈnɔt: te	il	ˈdʒor no
la	**notte,**	**il**	**giorno**
the	*night*	*the*	*day*

ˈsɛm pre	din ˈtor no	in	ˈdʒi ɾo	sta
sempre	**d'intorno**	**in**	**giro**	**sta.**
always	*all around*	*in*	*turn[s]*	*he is*

miʎ: ˈʎor	kuk: ˈkaɲ: ɲa	per	un	bar ˈbjɛ ɾe
Miglior	**cuccagna**	**per**	**un**	**barbiere,**
better	*feast*	*for*	*a*	*barber*

ˈvi ta	pju	ˈnɔ bi le
vita	**più**	**nobile,**
life	*more*	*noble*

nɔ   non   si ˈda
no,   non   si dà.
no   not   one can take up

ra ˈzɔ ɾi   e   ˈpet: ti ni
Rasori   e   pettini,
razors   and   combs

lan ˈtʃet: te   e   ˈfɔr bi tʃi
lancette   e   forbici
lancets   and   scissors

al   ˈmi o   ko ˈman do   ˈtut: to   kwi   sta
al   mio   comando   tutto   qui   sta.
at the   my   command   everything   here   is

vɛ   la   ri ˈsor sa
V'è   la   risorsa
there is   the   resource

ˈpɔ i   del   me ˈstje ɾe
poi   del   mestiere
besides   of the   occupation

ˈkol: la   don: ˈnet: ta
colla   donnetta...
with the   little lady

la   la   ran   ˈle ɾa
la   la   ran   lera—
la   la   tra   la

kol   ka va ˈlje ɾe
col   cavaliere...
with the   cavalier

la   la   ran   la
la   la   ran   la.
la   la   tra   la

ˈtut: ti   mi   ˈkje do no
Tutti   mi   chiedono,
everyone   me   calls

ˈtut: ti   mi   ˈvɔʎ: ʎo no
tutti   mi   vogliono,
everyone   me   wants

ˈdɔn: ne   ra ˈgat: tsi
donne,   ragazzi,
women   lads

ˈvɛk: ki   e   fan ˈtʃul: le
vecchi   e   fanciulle:
old men   and   young girls

kwa   la   par: ˈruk: ka
Qua   la   parrucca,
here   the   wig

ˈprɛ sto   la   ˈbar ba
presto   la   barba,
quick   the   shave

kwa la saŋ ˈgwiɲː ɲa
qua la sanguigna,
here the drawing of blood

ˈprɛ sto il biʎː ˈʎet̚ to
presto il biglietto!
quick the short letter

ˈe i ˈfi ga ɾo
Ehi, Figaro!
hey Figaro

a i ˈmɛ ke ˈfu ɾja
Ahimè! che furia!
alas what fury

a i ˈmɛ ke ˈfolː la
Ahimè! che folla!
alas what [a] crowd

ˈu no ˈalː la ˈvol ta
Uno alla volta
one at the time

per ka ɾi ˈta
per carità!
for pity's sake

ˈfi ga ɾo son kwa
Figaro! Son qua.
Figaro I am here

ˈe i ˈfi ga ɾo son kwa
Ehi, Figaro! Son qua.
hey Figaro I am here

ˈfi ga ɾo kwa ˈfi ga ɾo la
Figaro qua, Figaro là,
Figaro here Figaro there

ˈfi ga ɾo su ˈfi ga ɾo dʒu
Figaro su, Figaro giù!
Figaro above Figaro below

ˈpronto pron ˈtisː si mo son
Pronto prontissimo son
quick most quick I am

ˈko me il ˈful mi ne
come il fulmine;
like the lightning

ˈso no il fak ˈtɔ tum ˈdelː la tʃitː ˈta
sono il factotum della città!
I am the factotum of the city

a ˈbra vo ˈfi ga ɾo bra ˈvisː si mo
Ah bravo, Figaro, bravissimo!
ah well done Figaro very well done

a te for ˈtu na non maŋ ke ˈra
A te fortuna non mancherà.
to you [good] fortune not will be lacking

COSÌ FAN TUTTE
music: Wolfgang Amadeus Mozart
libretto: Lorenzo da Ponte

Donne mie, la fate a tanti

'dɔn: ne 'mi e la 'fa te a 'tan ti
Donne mie, la fate a tanti
ladies mine it you do to so many

ke se il ver vi 'dɛd: dʒo dir
che, se il ver vi deggio dir,
that if the truth you I must [to] tell

se si 'laɲ: ɲa no ʎi a 'man ti
se si lagnano gli amanti
if [they] complain the lovers

li kom: 'min tʃo a kom pa 'tir
li comincio a compatir.
them I begin to [to] sympathize with

'i o vɔ 'bɛ ne al 'sɛs: so 'vɔ stro
Io vo' bene al sesso vostro—
I [I] wish well to the sex yours

lo sa 'pe te oɲ: 'ɲun lo sa
lo sapete, ognun lo sà.
it you know everyone it knows

'oɲ: ɲi 'dʒor no ve lo 'mo stro
Ogni giorno ve lo mostro;
every day to you it I show

vi dɔ 'seɲ: ɲo da mi 'sta
vi do segno d'amistà.
to you I give sign of friendship

ma kwel 'far la
Ma quel farla
but that doing it

a 'tan ti e 'tan ti
a tanti e tanti,
to so many and so many

mav: vi 'liʃ: ʃe in ve ɾi 'ta
m'avvilisce in verità.
me disheartens in truth

'mil: le 'vɔl te il 'bran do 'pre zi
Mille volte il brando presi
thousand times the sword I took out

per sal 'var il 'vɔ stro o 'nor
per salvar il vostro onor;
in order to save the your honor

'mil: le 'vɔl te vi di 'fe zi
mille volte vi difesi
thousand times you I defended

'kol: la 'bok: ka e pju kol kɔr
colla bocca e più col cor.
with the mouth and more with the heart

ma	kwel	'far la	a	'tan ti	e	'tan ti
Ma	**quel**	**farla**	**a**	**tanti**	**e**	**tanti**
but	*that*	*doing it*	*to*	*so many*	*and*	*so many*

ε	un	vit: 'tsjet: to	sek: ka 'tor
è	**un**	**vizietto**	**seccator.**
is	*a*	*little vice*	*annoying*

'sjε te	'va ge	'sjε te	a 'ma bi li
Siete	**vaghe;**	**siete**	**amabili.**
you are	*lovely*	*you are*	*lovable*

pju	te 'zɔ ɾi	il	tʃεl	vi	djε
Più	**tesori**	**il**	**ciel**	**vi**	**diè,**
more	*treasures*	*the*	*heaven*	*to you*	*gave*

e	le	'grat: tsje	vi	tʃir 'kon da no
e	**le**	**grazie**	**vi**	**circondano**
and	*the*	*graces*	*you*	*[they] surround*

'dal: la	'tε sta	'si no 'a i	pjε
dalla	**testa**	**sino ai**	**piè.**
from the	*head*	*as far as to the*	*feet*

ma	la	'fa te	a	'tan ti	e	'tan ti
Ma,	**la**	**fate**	**a**	**tanti**	**e**	**tanti**
but	*it*	*you do*	*to*	*so many*	*and*	*so many*

ke	kre 'di bi le	non	ε
che	**credibile**	**non**	**è.**
that	*believable*	*not*	*it is*

'i o	vɔ	'bε ne	al	'sεs: so	'vɔ stro
Io	**vo'**	**bene**	**al**	**sesso**	**vostro;**
I	*[I] wish*	*well*	*to the*	*sex*	*yours*

ve	lo	'mo stro
ve	**lo**	**mostro.**
to you	*it*	*I show*

'mil: le	'vɔl te	il	'bran do	'pre zi
Mille	**volte**	**il**	**brando**	**presi;**
thousand	*times*	*the*	*sword*	*I took out*

vi	di 'fe zi
vi	**difesi.**
you	*I defended*

gran	te 'zɔ ɾi	il	tʃεl	vi	djε
Gran	**tesori**	**il**	**ciel**	**vi**	**diè,**
great	*treasures*	*the*	*heaven*	*to you*	*gave*

'si no 'a i	pjε
sino ai	**piè.**
as far as to the	*feet*

ma	la	'fa te	a	'tan ti	e	'tan ti
Ma,	**la**	**fate**	**a**	**tanti**	**e**	**tanti**
but	*it*	*you do*	*to*	*so many*	*and*	*so many*

ke	se	'gri da no	ʎi	a 'man ti
che	**se**	**gridano**	**gli**	**amanti**
that	*if*	*[they] protest*	*the*	*lovers*

'an: no	'tʃεr to	un	gran	per 'ke
hanno	**certo**	**un**	**gran**	**perchè.**
they have	*certainly*	*a*	*great*	*reason*

DON GIOVANNI

music: Wolfgang Amadeus Mozart
libretto: Lorenzo da Ponte (after Giovanni Bertati's libretto for Giuseppe Gazzaniga's *Il convitato di pietra*; also after the Don Juan legends)

Fin ch'han dal vino

fiŋ ˈkan	dal		ˈvi no	ˈkal da	la	ˈtɛ sta
Fin ch'han	**dal**		**vino**	**calda**	**la**	**testa,**
until they have	*from the*		*wine*	*hot*	*the*	*head*

ˈu na	gran	ˈfɛ sta	fa	pre pa ˈɾar
una	**gran**	**festa**	**fa'**	**preparar.**
a	*big*	*party*	*make*	*to prepare*

se	ˈtrɔ vi	in	ˈpjat: tsa	ˈkwal ke	ra ˈgat: tsa
Se	**trovi**	**in**	**piazza**	**qualche**	**ragazza,**
if	*you find*	*in*	*town square*	*some*	*girl*

ˈte ko	aŋ ˈkor	ˈkwel: la	ˈtʃer ka	me ˈnar	
teco	**ancor**	**quella**	**cerca**	**menar.**	
you with	*also*	*that one*	*try*	*to bring*	

ˈsɛn tsa	al ˈkun	ˈor di ne	la	ˈdan tsa	ˈsi a
Senza	**alcun**	**ordine**	**la**	**danza**	**sia,**
without	*any*	*order*	*the*	*dance*	*let be*

kil	mi nu ˈet: to	ki	la	fol: ˈli a
chi'l	**minuetto,**	**chi**	**la**	**follia,**
some the	*minuet*	*some*	*the*	*follia*

ki	la le ˈman: na	fa ˈɾa i	bal: ˈlar
chi	**l'alemanna**	**farai**	**ballar.**
some	*the allemande*	*you will make*	*to dance*

e ˈdi o	fra ˈtan to	dal: ˈlal tro	ˈkan to	
Ed io	**fra tanto**	**dall'altro**	**canto**	
and I	*in the meantime*	*from the other*	*corner*	

kon	ˈkwe sta	e	ˈkwel: la	vɔ	a mo ɾed: ˈdʒar
con	**questa**	**e**	**quella**	**vo'**	**amoreggiar.**
with	*this girl*	*and*	*that girl*	*I want*	*to flirt*

a	la	ˈmi a	ˈli sta	do ˈman	mat: ˈti na
Ah,	**la**	**mia**	**lista**	**doman**	**mattina**
ah	*the*	*my*	*list*	*tomorrow*	*morning*

ˈdu na	de ˈtʃi na	ˈdɛ vi	a u men ˈtar
d'una	**decina**	**devi**	**aumentar.**
by a	*ten or so*	*you ought*	*to lengthen*

Deh, vieni alla finestra

dɛ   'vjɛ ni   'al: la   fi 'nɛ stra
Deh,   vieni   alla   finestra,
please   come   to the   window

o   'mi o   te 'zɔ ɾo
o   mio   tesoro.
o   my   treasure

dɛ   'vjɛ ni   a   kon so 'lar
Deh,   vieni   a   consolar
please   come   to   [to] console

il   'pjan to   'mi o
il   pianto   mio.
the   weeping   mine

se   'ne gi   a   me   di   dar
Se   neghi   a   me   di   dar
if   you deny   to   me   of   to give

'kwal ke   ri 'stɔ ɾo
qualche   ristoro,
some   solace

da 'van ti   'aʎ: ʎi   'ɔk: ki   'twɔ i
davanti   agli   occhi   tuoi
in front of   [at] the   eyes   yours

mo 'ɾir   vɔʎ: 'ʎi o
morir   vogl'io.
to die   want I

tu   'ka i   la   'bok: ka
Tu   ch'hai   la   bocca
you   who have   the   mouth

'dol tʃe   pju   ke   il   'mjɛ le
dolce   più   che   il   miele—
sweet   more   than   the   honey

tu   ke   il   'tsuk: ke ɾo   'pɔr ti
tu   che   il   zucchero   porti
you   who   the   sugar   bear

in   'mɛd: dzo   al   'kɔ ɾe
in   mezzo   al   core—
in   middle   of the   heart

non   'ɛs: ser   'dʒɔ ja   'mi a
non   esser,   gioia   mia,
not   be   joy   mine

kon   me   kru 'dɛ le
con   me   crudele.
with   me   cruel

'laʃ: ʃa ti   al 'men   ve 'der
Lasciati   almen   veder,
let yourself   at least   to see

'mi o   bɛl: la 'mo ɾe
mio   bell'amore.
my   beautiful love

DON PASQUALE

music: Gaetano Donizetti

libretto: Gaetano Donizetti and Giovanni Ruffini (after Aneli's libretto for Pavesi's *Ser Marc' Antonio*)

Bella siccome un angelo

'bɛl: la   sik: 'ko me   un   'an dʒe lo
Bella   siccome   un   angelo
beautiful   as   an   angel

in   'tɛr: ra   pel: le 'gri no
in   terra   pellegrino,
on   earth   pilgrim

'fre ska   sik: 'ko me   il   'dʒiʎ: ʎo
fresca   siccome   il   giglio
fresh   as   the   lily

ke   'sa pre   sul   mat: 'ti no
che   s'apre   sul   mattino,
which   opens up   upon the   morning

'ɔk: kjo   ke   'par la   e   'ri de
occhio   che   parla   e   ride,
eye   which   speaks   and   laughs

'zgwar do   ke   i   kɔr   kon 'kwi de
sguardo   che   i   cor   conquide,
glance   which   the   hearts   conquers

'kjɔ ma   ke   'vin tʃe   'lɛ ba no
chioma   che   vince   l'ebano,
hair   which   surpasses   the ebony

sor: 'ri zo   iŋ kan ta 'tor
sorriso   incantator...
smile   enchanting

'al ma   in: no 'tʃɛn te   in 'dʒɛ nu a
Alma   innocente,   ingenua,
soul   innocent   ingenuous

ke   se me 'dez ma   iɲ: 'ɲɔ ra
che   sè medesma   ignora,
which   she herself   ignores

mo 'dɛ stja   im pa ɾed: 'dʒa bi le
modestia   impareggiabile,
modesty   incomparable

bon 'ta   ke   vin: na 'mo ɾa
bontà   che   v'innamora...
goodness   which   you causes to fall in love

'a i   'mi ze ɾi   pje 'to za
Ai   miseri   pietosa,
to the   poverty-stricken   merciful

dʒen 'til   'dol tʃe   a mo 'ro za
gentil,   dolce,   amorosa...
gentle   sweet   affectionate

il   tʃɛl   la   'fat: ta   'naʃ: ʃe ɾe
Il   ciel   l'ha   fatta   nascere
the   heaven her has made   to be born

per   far   be 'a to   uŋ   kɔr
per   far   beato   un   cor.
in order to make happy   a   heart

EDGAR

music: Giacomo Puccini

libretto: Ferdinando Fontana (after *La Coupe et les Lèvres,* a verse drama by Alfred de Musset)

Questo amor, vergogna mia

'kwe sto · a 'mor   ver 'goɲ: ɲa   'mi a
Questo   amor,   vergogna   mia,
this   love   shame   mine

'i o   spet: 'tsar   skor 'dar   vor: 'rɛ i
io   spezzar,   scordar   vorrei;
I   to break off to forget   [I] should like

ma   du 'nɔr: ri da   ma 'li a
ma   d'un' orrida   malìa
but   of a horrible   enchantment

'so no   'skja vi   i   'sɛn si   'mjɛ i
sono   schiavi   i   sensi   miei.
are   slaves   the senses   mine

'mil: le   'vɔl te   al   tʃɛl
Mille   volte   al   ciel
thousand times   to the heaven

dʒu 'ɾa i   di   fud: 'dʒir la
giurai   di   fuggirla,
I swore   of   to flee from her

e   a   'lɛ i   tor 'na i
e   a   lei   tornai!
and   to   her   I returned

'el: la   'ri de   del   'mi o   'pjan to
Ella   ride   del   mio   pianto,
she   laughs   about the my   weeping

e 'di o   vil   kol   'kwɔ ɾe   in 'fran to
ed io,   vil,   col   cuore   infranto,
and I   wretched with the heart   broken

'a i   'swɔ i   'pjɛ di   mi   pro 'stɛr no
ai   suoi   piedi   mi   prosterno.
at the her   feet   myself I prostrate

'el: la   'ri de   del   'mi o   'pjan to
Ella   ride   del   mio   pianto;
she   laughs   about the my   weeping

del   'mi o   'zdeɲ: ɲo   si fa   'sker no
del   mio   sdegno   si fa   scherno.
of the my   disdain   she makes mockery

e 'di o   vil   kol   'kwɔ ɾe   in 'fran to
Ed io,   vil,   col   cuore   infranto,
and I   wretched with the heart   broken

'a i   'swɔ i   'pjɛ di   mi   pro 'stɛr no
ai   **suoi**   **piedi**   **mi**   **prosterno.**
at the   *her*   *feet*   *myself*   *I prostrate*

e   'lɛ i   'so la   'i o   'soɲ: ɲo
E   **lei**   **sola**   **io**   **sogno,**
and   *her*   *only*   *I*   *[I] dream about*

'bra mo
bramo!
[I] desire

a   zven 'tu ɾa
Ah   **sventura!**
ah   *misfortune*

'i o   'la mo   'la mo
Io   **l'amo!**   **L'amo!**
I   *her I love*   *her I love*

L'ELISIR D'AMORE

music: Gaetano Donizetti
libretto: Felice Romani (after Eugène Scribe's libretto for Daniel-François Auber's *Le Philtre*)

Come Paride vezzoso

'ko me   'pa ɾi de   vet: 'tso zo   'pɔr se   il   'po mo
Come   **Paride**   **vezzoso**   **porse**   **il**   **pomo**
Like   *Paris*   *charming*   *offered*   *the*   *apple*

'al: la   pju   'bɛl: la
alla   **più**   **bella,**
to the   *most*   *beautiful woman*

'mi a   di 'lɛt: ta   vil: la 'nɛl: la
mia   **diletta**   **villanella,**
my   *beloved*   *peasant girl*

'i o   ti   'pɔr go   'kwe sti   fjor
io   **ti**   **porgo**   **questi**   **fior.**
I   *to you*   *[I] offer*   *these*   *flowers*

ma   di   'lu i   pju   glo ɾi 'o zo
Ma   **di**   **lui**   **più**   **glorioso,**
but   *than*   *he*   *more*   *glorious*

pju   di   'lu i   fe 'li tʃe   'i o   'so no
più   **di**   **lui**   **felice**   **io**   **sono,**
more   *than*   *he*   *happy*   *I*   *[I] am*

po i 'ke   in   'prɛ mjo   del   'mi o   'do no
poichè   **in**   **premio**   **del**   **mio**   **dono**
since   *in*   *reward*   *of the*   *my*   *gift*

ne   ri 'pɔr to
ne   **riporto**
from it   *I take back*

il   'tu o   bɛl   kɔr
il   **tuo**   **bel**   **cor.**
the   *your*   *beautiful*   *heart*

'veg: go   'kja ɾo   in   kwel   vi 'zi no
Veggo   chiaro   in   quel   visino
I see   clear   in   that   little face

'ki o   fɔ   'brɛt: tʃa   nel   'tu o   'pɛt: to
ch'io   fo   breccia   nel   tuo   petto.
that I   [I] make   breach   in the   your   breast

non   ɛ   'kɔ za   sor pren 'dɛn te
Non   è   cosa   sorprendente;
not   it is   thing   surprising

son   ga 'lan te   e   son   sar 'dʒɛn te
son   galante,   e   son   sargente.
I am   galant   and   I am   sergeant

non   va   'bɛl: la   ke   re 'zi sta
Non   v'ha   bella   che   resista
not   there is   beautiful woman   who   may resist

'al: la   'vi sta   dun   tʃi 'mjɛ ɾo
alla   vista   d'un   cimiero;
at the   sight   of a   crest

'tʃe de   a   'mar te   'di o   gwer: 'rjɛ ɾo
cede   a   Marte,   Dio   guerriero,
yields   to   Mars   God   warrior

fin   la   'ma dre   del: la 'mor
fin   la   madre   dell'Amor.
even   the   mother   of Love

LA FANCIULLA DEL WEST

music: Giacomo Puccini
libretto: Carlo Zangarini and Guelfo Civinini (after the play by David Belasco)

Minnie, dalla mia casa son partito

'min: ni   'dal: la   'mi a   'ka za   son par 'ti to
Minnie,   dalla   mia   casa   son partito
Minnie   from the   my   house   I have departed

ke   ɛ   la   'da i   'mon ti
che   è   là   dai   monti,
which   is   over there   beyond the   mountains

'so pra   un   'al tro   'ma ɾe
sopra   un   altro   mare.
over   an   other   sea

non   un   rim 'pjan to   'min: ni
Non   un   rimpianto,   Minnie,
not   a   regret   Minnie

ma   se 'gwi to
m'ha   seguito;
me has   followed

non   un   rim 'pjan to   vi   po 'te a   laʃ: 'ʃa ɾe
non   un   rimpianto   vi   potea   lasciare!
not   a   regret   there   I was able   to leave

nes: ˈsu no   ˈma i   ma ˈmɔ
Nessuno   **mai**   **m'amò;**
no one   *ever*   *me loved*

nes: ˈsu no   ɔ   a ˈma to
nessuno   **ho**   **amato.**
no one   *I have*   *loved*

nes: ˈsu na   ˈkɔ za   ˈma i   mi   djɛ   pja ˈtʃe ɾe
Nessuna   **cosa**   **mai**   **mi**   **diè**   **piacere!**
no   *thing*   *ever*   *to me*   *gave*   *pleasure*

ˈkju do   nel   ˈpɛt: to   un   kwɔr   di   bi skat: ˈtsjɛ ɾe
Chiudo   **nel**   **petto**   **un**   **cuor**   **di**   **biscazziere,**
I enclose   *in the*   *breast*   *a*   *heart*   *of*   *gambler*

a ˈma ɾo   av: ve le ˈna to
amaro,   **avvelenato,**
bitter   *poisoned*

ke   ˈri de   del: la ˈmo ɾe   e   del   de ˈsti no
che   **ride**   **dell'amore**   **e**   **del**   **destino.**
which   *laughs*   *about the love*   *and*   *about the*   *fate*

mi son ˈmes: so   iŋ   kam: ˈmi no
Mi son messo   **in**   **cammino**
I set out   *on*   *road*

at: ˈtrat: to   sol   dal   faʃ: ˈʃi no   del: ˈlɔ ɾo
attratto   **sol**   **dal**   **fascino**   **dell'oro.**
attracted   *only*   *by the*   *fascination*   *of the gold*

ɛ   ˈkwe sto   il   ˈso lo
È   **questo**   **il**   **solo**
is   *this*   *the*   *only [thing]*

ke   non   ma   iŋ ɡan: ˈna to
che   **non**   **m'ha**   **ingannato.**
which   *not*   *me has*   *deceived*

or   per   un   ˈba tʃo   ˈtu o   ˈdʒɛt: to
Or   **per**   **un**   **bacio**   **tuo**   **getto**
now   *for*   *a*   *kiss*   *yours*   *I throw away*

un   te ˈzɔ ɾo
un   **tesoro!**
a   *treasure*

LA GIOCONDA

music: Amilcare Ponchielli
libretto: "Tobia Gorrio," a pseudonym for Arrigo Boito (after *Angelo, Tyran de Padoue*, a drama by Victor Hugo)

Ah! Pescator

a	pe ska ˈtor	afː ˈfon da	ˈle ska
Ah!	**Pescator,**	**affonda**	**l'esca;**
ah	*fisherman*	*sink*	*the bait*

a	te	ˈlon da	ˈsi a	fe ˈdel
a	**te**	**l'onda**	**sia**	**fedel.**
to	*you*	*the wave*	*may be*	*faithful*

ˈljɛ ta	ˈse ɾa	e	ˈbwɔ na	ˈpe ska
Lieta	**sera**	**e**	**buona**	**pesca**
happy	*evening*	*and*	*good*	*fishing*

ti	pro ˈmetː te	il	ˈma ɾe	il	tʃɛl
ti	**promette**	**il**	**mare,**	**il**	**ciel.**
to you	*promises*	*the*	*sea*	*the*	*sky*

va	traŋ ˈkwilː la	kan ti ˈlɛ na
Va,	**tranquilla**	**cantilena,**
go	*tranquil*	*lullaby*

per	ladː ˈdʒurː ra	imː men si ˈta
per	**l'azzurra**	**immensità.**
through	*the blue*	*vastness*

a	ˈu na	ˈpla tʃi da	si ˈɾɛ na
Ah!	**una**	**placida**	**sirena**
ah	*a*	*placid*	*siren*

ˈnelː la	ˈre te	ka ske ˈɾa
nella	**rete**	**cascherà.**
into the	*net*	*will fall*

ˈspi a	ˈko i	ful ˈmi ne i	ˈtwɔ i	ˈzgwar di	akː ˈkɔr ti
(Spia	**coi**	**fulminei**	**tuoi**	**sguardi**	**accorti,**
spy	*with the*	*lightning*	*your*	*glances*	*cunning*

e	fra	le	ˈtɛ ne bre	ˈkon ta	i	ˈtwɔ i	ˈmɔr ti
e	**fra**	**le**	**tenebre**	**conta**	**i**	**tuoi**	**morti.**
and	*among*	*the*	*darknesses*	*count*	*the*	*your*	*dead ones*

si	da	kwe ˈsti zo la	de ˈzɛr ta	e	ˈbru na
Sì,	**da**	**quest'isola**	**deserta**	**e**	**bruna**
yes	*from*	*this island*	*deserted*	*and*	*dark*

or	ˈde ve	ˈsor dʒe ɾe	la	ˈtu a	for ˈtu na
or	**deve**	**sorgere**	**la**	**tua**	**fortuna.**
now	*ought*	*to rise*	*the*	*your*	*fortune*

sta	iŋ	ˈgwar dja	e	il	ˈra pi do	so ˈspɛtː to	ˈzvi a
Sta	**in**	**guardia!**	**e**	**il**	**rapido**	**sospetto**	**svia,**
be	*on*	*guard*	*and*	*the*	*quick*	*suspicion*	*divert*

e	ˈri di	e	ˈvi dʒi la	e	ˈkan ta
e	**ridi**	**e**	**vigila**	**e**	**canta**
and	*laugh*	*and*	*be on the alert*	*and*	*sing*

e	ˈspi a
e	**spia!)**
and	*spy*

a   'bril: la   've ne ɾe   se 're na
Ah!   brilla   Venere   serena
ah   shines   Venus   serene

in   un   tʃɛl   di   vo lut: 'ta
in   un   ciel   di   voluttà;
in   a   heaven   of   voluptuousness

'u na   'ful dʒi da   si 'rɛ na
una   fulgida   sirena
a   resplendent   siren

'nel: la   're te   ka ske 'ɾa
nella   rete   cascherà.
into the   net   will fall

la   si 'rɛ na   'nel: la   're te   ka ske 'ɾa
La   sirena   nella   rete   cascherà,
the   siren   into the   net   will fall

si   ka ske 'ɾa
sì,   cascherà!
yes   she will fall

LE NOZZE DI FIGARO

music: Wolfgang Amadeus Mozart
libretto: Lorenzo da Ponte (after *La Folle Journée, ou Le Mariage de Figaro*, a comedy by Pierre Augustin Caron de Beaumarchais)

Hai già vinta la causa!... Vedrò mentr'io sospiro

'a i   dʒa   'vin ta   la   'ka u za
Hai   già   vinta   la   causa!
you have   already   won   the   case

'kɔ za   'sɛn to
Cosa   sento!
what   I hear

in   kwal   'lat: tʃo   'i o   ka 'de a
In   qual   laccio   io   cadea?
in   what   trap   I   fell

'pɛr fi di
Perfidi!
traitors

'i o   'vɔʎ: ʎo   di   tal   'mɔ do   pu 'nir vi
Io   voglio   di   tal   modo   punirvi;
I   [I] want   in   such   manner   to punish you

a   pja 'tʃer   'mi o   la   sen 'tɛn tsa   sa 'ra
a   piacer   mio   la   sentenza   sarà.
at   pleasure   mine   the   judgement   will be

ma   'se i   pa 'gas: se   la   'vɛk: kja   pre ten 'dɛn te
Ma   s'ei   pagasse   la   vecchia   pretendente?
but   if he   should pay   the   old   claimant

pa 'gar la   in   kwal   man 'jɛ ɾa
Pargarla!   In   qual   maniera?
to pay her   in   what   manner

e   'pɔ i   vɛ   an 'tɔ njo
E   poi   v'è   Antonio,
and   then   there is   Antonio

ke   a un iŋ 'kɔɲː ɲi to   'fi ga ɾo
che   a un incognito   Figaro
who   to the uneducated   Figaro

ri 'ku za   di   'da ɾe   'u na   ni 'po te   in   ma tri 'mɔ njo
ricusa   di   dare   una   nipote   in   matrimonio.
refuses   of   to give   a   niece   in   marriage

kol ti 'van do   lor 'goʎː ʎo
Coltivando   l'orgoglio
cultivating   the pride

di   'kwe sto   men te 'kat: to
di   questo   mentecatto,
of   this   fool

'tut: to   'dʒo va   a   un   rad: 'dʒi ɾo
tutto   giova   a   un   raggiro.
everything   is useful   for   an   intrigue

il   'kol po   ɛ   'fat: to
Il   colpo   è   fatto.
the   move   is   made

ve 'drɔ   men 'tri o   so 'spi ɾo
Vedrò,   mentri'io   sospiro,
I shall see   while I   [I] sigh for

fe 'li tʃe   un   'sɛr vo   'mi o
felice   un   servo   mio?
happy   a   servant   mine

e   un   bɛn   ke   in 'van   de 'zi o
E   un   ben   che   invan   desio
and   a   dear one   whom   in vain   I desire

'e i   pos: se 'der   do 'vra
ei   posseder   dovrà?
he   to possess   shall be permitted

ve 'drɔ   per   man   da 'mo ɾe
Vedrò   per   man   d'amore,
I shall see   through   hand   of love

u 'ni ta   a   un   'vi le   od: 'dʒet: to
unita   a   un   vile   oggetto
united   to   a   miserable   object

ki   in   me   de 'stɔ   un   af: 'fɛt: to
chi   in   me   destò   un   affetto,
one who   in   me   awakened   an   affection

ke   per   me   'pɔ i   non   a
che   per   me   poi   non   ha?
which   for   me   then   not   she has

ve 'drɔ   ke   un   bɛn   'ki o   de 'zi o
Vedrò   che   un   ben   ch'io   desio,
I shall see   that   a   dear one   whom I   [I] desire

'e i   pos: se 'der   do 'vra
ei   posseder   dovrà?
he   to possess   shall be permitted

ve 'drɔ
Vedrò?
I shall see

a   nɔ   laʃ: 'ʃar ti   in   'pa tʃe
Ah   no!   lasciarti   in   pace
ah   no   to leave you   in   peace

non   vɔ   'kwe sto   kon 'tɛn to
non   vo'   questo   contento.
not   I want   this   satisfaction

tu   non   naʃ: 'ʃe sti   a u 'da tʃe
Tu   non   nascesti,   audace,
you   not   were born   audacious one

per   'da ɾe   a   me   tor 'men to
per   dare   a   me   tormento,
for   to give   to   me   torment

e   'for se   aŋ 'kor   per   'ri de ɾe
e   forse   ancor   per   ridere
and   perhaps   also   for   to laugh

di   'mi a   in fe li tʃi 'ta
di   mia   infelicità.
about   my   unhappiness

dʒa   la   spe 'ran tsa   'so la
Già   la   speranza   sola
already   the   hope   alone

'del: le   ven 'det: te   'mi e
delle   vendette   mie
of the   vengeances   mine

kwes 'ta ni ma   kon 'so la
quest'anima   consola,
this soul   consoles

e   dʒu bi 'lar   mi   fa
e   giubilar   mi   fa.
and   to rejoice   me   makes

I PAGLIACCI

music: Ruggero Leoncavallo
libretto: Ruggero Leoncavallo (based on a legal case his father heard as a judge)

Si può? Si può?

si pwɔ
Si può?
is it permitted [to come in]

siɲ: ˈɲo ɾe	siɲ: ˈɲo ɾi
Signore!	**Signori!**
ladies	*gentlemen*

sku ˈza te mi	se	da sol	mi	pre ˈzɛn to
Scusatemi	**se**	**da sol**	**mi**	**presento.**
excuse me	*if*	*by myself alone*	*myself*	*I present*

ˈi o	ˈso no	il	ˈprɔ lo go
Io	**sono**	**il**	**Prologo.**
I	*[I] am*	*the*	*Prologue*

po i ˈke	in	iʃ: ˈʃe na	aŋ ˈkor
Poichè	**in**	**iscena**	**ancor**
since	*on*	*stage*	*again*

le	an ˈti ke	ˈma ske ɾe
le	**antiche**	**maschere**
the	*ancient*	*maskers*

ˈmet: te	la u ˈto ɾe
mette	**l'autore,**
puts	*the author*

in	ˈpar te	ˈe i	vwɔl	ri ˈprɛn de ɾe
in	**parte**	**ei**	**vuol**	**riprendere**
in	*part*	*he*	*wishes*	*to take up again*

le	ˈvɛk: kje	u ˈzan tse
le	**vecchie**	**usanze,**
the	*old*	*customs*

e	a	ˈvo i	di ˈnwɔ vo	in ˈvi a mi
e	**a**	**voi**	**di nuovo**	**inviami.**
and	*to*	*you*	*again*	*he dispatches me*

ma	non	per	ˈdir vi	ˈko me	ˈpri a
Ma	**non**	**per**	**dirvi**	**come**	**pria:**
but	*not*	*for*	*to tell you*	*as*	*before*

le	ˈla kri me	ke	ˈno i	ver ˈsjam	son	ˈfal se
«Le	**lacrime**	**che**	**noi**	**versiam**	**son**	**false!**
the	*tears*	*that*	*we*	*[we] shed*	*are*	*false*

ˈdeʎ: ʎi	ˈspa zi mi	e	de	ˈnɔ stri	mar ˈtir
Degli	**spasimi**	**e**	**de'**	**nostri**	**martir**
about the	*pangs of pain*	*and*	*of [the]*	*our*	*agonies*

non	al: lar ˈma te vi
non	**allarmatevi!»**
not	*alarm yourselves*

nɔ	la u ˈto ɾe	a	tʃer ˈka to	in ˈve tʃe
No!	**L'autore**	**ha**	**cercato**	**invece**
no	*the author*	*has*	*looked for*	*rather*

24

'pin dʒer vi   'u no   'skwar tʃo   di   'vi ta
pingervi   **uno**   **squarcio**   **di**   **vita.**
painting for you   *an*   *excerpt*   *from*   *life*

'eʎːʎi   a   per   'masː si ma   sol
Egli   **ha**   **per**   **massima**   **sol**
he   *has*   *for*   *maxim*   *only*

ke   lar 'ti sta   ɛ   un   wɔm
che   **l'artista**   **è**   **un**   **uom**
that   *the artist*   *is*   *a*   *man*

e   ke   per   ʎi   'wɔ mi ni   'skri ve ɾe   'e i   'dɛ ve
e   **che**   **per**   **gli**   **uomini**   **scrivere**   **ei**   **deve.**
and   *that*   *for*   *the*   *men*   *to write*   *he*   *[he] must*

e dal   've ɾo   i spi 'ra va si
Ed al   **vero**   **ispiravasi.**
and by the   *truth*   *he was inspired*

un   'ni do   di   me 'mɔ rje   in   'fon do   a   'la ni ma
Un   **nido**   **di**   **memorie**   **in**   **fondo**   **a**   **l'anima**
a   *nest*   *of*   *memories*   *in*   *depth*   *at*   *the soul*

kan 'ta va   un   'dʒor no
cantava   ʲ   **un**   **giorno,**
sang   *one*   *day*

e 'de i   kon   've ɾe   'la kri me   'skrisː se
ed ei   **con**   **vere**   **lacrime**   **scrisse,**
and he   *with*   *real*   *tears*   *wrote*

e   i   siŋ 'ɡjotː tsi   il   'tɛm po   ʎi   batː 'te va no
e   **i**   **singhiozzi**   **il**   **tempo**   **gli**   **battevano!**
and   *the*   *sobs*   *the*   *time*   *for him*   *beat*

'duŋ kwe   ve 'dre te   a 'mar
Dunque,   **vedrete**   **amar**
therefore   *you will see*   *loving*

si   'ko me   'sa ma no   ʎi   'ɛsː se ɾi   u 'ma ni
sì   **come**   **s'amano**   **gli**   **esseri**   **umani;**
as   *like*   *[they] love each other*   *the*   *beings*   *human*

ve 'dre te   delː 'lɔ djo   i   'tri sti   'frutː ti
vedrete   **dell'odio**   **i**   **tristi**   **frutti.**
you will see   *of the hate*   *the*   *sad*   *fruits*

del   do 'lor   ʎi   'spa zi mi
Del   **dolor**   **gli**   **spasimi,**
of the   *sorrow*   *the*   *pangs of pain*

'ur li   di   'rabː bja   u 'dre te
urli   **di**   **rabbia**   **udrete,**
howls   *of*   *rage*   *you will hear*

e   'ri za   'tʃi ni ke
e   **risa**   **ciniche!**
and   *laughter*   *cynical*

e   'vo i   pjutː 'tɔ sto   ke   le   'nɔ stre
E   **voi,**   **piuttosto**   **che**   **le**   **nostre**
and   *you*   *rather*   *than*   *the*   *our*

'pɔ ve ɾe   ɡabː 'ba ne   di sti 'o ni
povere   **gabbane**   **d'istrioni,**
poor   *overcoats*   *of actors*

le   nɔ 'stra ni me   kon si de 'ra te
le   nostr'anime   considerate,
the   our souls   consider

pɔ i 'ke   sjam   'wɔ mi ni   di   'kar ne   e   'dɔs: sa
poichè siam   uomini   di   carne   e   d'ossa,
because we are men   of   flesh   and of bones

e   ke   di   kwe 'stɔr fa no   'mon do
e   che   di   quest'orfano   mondo
and because of   this parentless   world

al   'pa ɾi   di   'vo i   spi 'ɾja mo   'la e ɾe
al   pari   di   voi   spiriamo   l'aere!
at the equal of   you   we breathe   the air

il   kon 'tʃɛt: to   vi   'dis: si
Il   concetto   vi   dissi...
the concept   to you I told

or   a skol 'ta te   ko 'meʎ: ʎi   ɛ   'zvɔl to
or   ascoltate   com'egli   è   svolto.
now listen   how it   is   unwound

an 'djam
Andiam.
let's go

iŋ ko min 'tʃa te
Incominciate!
begin

I PURITANI

music: Vincenzo Bellini
libretto: Count Carlo Pepoli (after *Têtes Rondes et Cavaliers,* a play by Jacques-Arsène Ancelot and Joseph Xavier Boniface)

Ah! per sempre io ti perdei

or   'do ve   'fug: go   'i o   'ma i
Or   dove   fuggo   io   mai?
now where [I] flee   I   ever

'do ve   'ma i   'tʃɛ lo   ʎi   or: 'rɛn di   af: 'fan: ni   'mjɛ i
Dove   mai   celo   gli   orrendi   affanni   miei?
where ever I hide   the   horrible   anguishes   mine

'ko me   'kwe i   'kan ti   mi   ri 'swɔ na no
Come   quei   canti   mi   risuonano
how those songs to me [they] resonate

al: 'lal ma   a 'ma ɾi   'pjan ti
all'alma   amari   pianti!
to the soul bitter   tears

o   el 'vi ɾa   o   'mi o   so 'spir   so 'a ve
O   Elvira,   o   mio   sospir   soave,
o   Elvira   o   my   desired one   gentle

per   ˈsɛm pre   ˈi o   ti   per ˈde i
per   sempre   io   ti   perdei!
for   always   I   you   [I] lost

ˈsɛn tsa   ˈspɛ me   e da ˈmor
Senza   speme   ed amor,
without   hope   and love

iŋ   ˈkwe sta   ˈvi ta   or   ke   ri ˈma ne   a   me
in   questa   vita   or   che   rimane   a   me?
in   this   life   now   what   remains   to   me

a   per   ˈsɛm pre   ˈi o   ti   per ˈde i
Ah!   per   sempre   io   ti   perdei,
ah   for   always   I   you   [I] lost

fjor   da ˈmo ɾe   o   ˈmi a   spe ˈɾan tsa
fior   d'amore,   o   mia   speranza.
flower   of love   o   my   hope

a   la   ˈvi ta   ke   ma ˈvan tsa
Ah!   la   vita   che   m'avanza
ah   the   life   which   to me is left

sa ˈɾa   ˈpjɛ na   di   do ˈlor
sarà   piena   di   dolor!
will be   full   of   sorrow

ˈkwan do   erː ˈra i   per   ˈanː ni   e ˈdanː ni
Quando   errai   per   anni   ed anni
when   I wandered   for   years   and years

in   po ˈter   ˈdelː la   ven ˈtu ɾa
in   poter   della   ventura,
in   power   of the   chance

ˈi o   sfi ˈda i   ʃa ˈgu ɾa   e   afː ˈfanː ni
io   sfidai   sciagura   e   affanni
I   [I] defied   misfortune   and   sufferings

ˈnelː la   ˈspɛ me   del   ˈtu o   a ˈmor
nella   speme   del   tuo   amor.
in the   hope   of the   your   love

RIGOLETTO

music: Giuseppe Verdi
libretto: Francesco Maria Piave (after Victor Hugo's drama *Le Roi s' Amuse*)

Pari siamo!

ˈpa ɾi   ˈsja mo
Pari   siamo!
equal   we are

ˈi o   la   ˈliŋ gwa   ˈeʎː ʎi   a   il   puɲː ˈɲa le
Io   la   lingua;   egli   ha   il   pugnale.
I   the   tongue   he   has   the   dagger

ˈlwɔ mo   son   ˈi o   ke   ˈri de
L'uomo   son   io   che   ride;
the man   [I] am   I   who   laughs

'e i kwel ke 'speɲ: ɲe
ei quel che spegne!
he that one who kills

kwel 'vɛk: kjo ma le 'di va mi
Quel vecchio maledivami!
that old man cursed me

o 'wɔ mi ni o na 'tu ɾa
O uomini! O natura!
oh mankind oh nature

vil ʃel: le 'ɾa to mi fa 'tʃe ste 'vo i
Vil scellerato mi faceste voi!
miserable villain me [you] made you

o 'rab: bja 'ɛs: ser dif: 'for me
Oh rabbia! esser difforme!
oh fury to be deformed

o 'rab: bja 'ɛs: ser buf: 'fo ne
Oh rabbia! esser buffone!
oh fury to be jester

non do 'ver non po 'ter
Non dover, non poter
not to be permitted not to be able

'al tro ke 'ri de ɾe
altro che ridere!
other than to laugh

il re 'tad: dʒo 'doɲ: ɲi wɔm mɛ 'tɔl to
Il retaggio d'ogni uom m'è tolto—
the birthright of every man from me is taken away

il 'pjan to
il pianto.
the weeping

'kwe sto pa 'dro ne 'mi o 'dʒo vin
Questo padrone mio — giovin,
this master mine young

dʒo 'kon do si pos: 'sɛn te 'bɛl: lo
giocondo, sì possente, bello —
merry so powerful handsome

son: nek: 'kjan do mi 'di tʃe
sonnecchiando mi dice:
drowsing to me says

fa 'ki o 'ri da buf: 'fo ne
Fa ch'io rida, buffone.
make that I [I] may laugh jester

for 'tsar mi 'dɛd: dʒo e 'far lo
Forzarmi deggio e farlo!
to force myself I must and to do it

o dan: na 'tsjo ne
Oh dannazione!
oh damnation

'ɔ djo a 'vo i kor ti 'dʒa ni sker ni 'to ɾi
Odio a voi, cortigiani schernitori!
hatred to you courtiers scornful

'kwan ta   in   'mɔr der vi   ɔ   'dʒɔ ja
Quanta   **in**   **mordervi**   **ho**   **gioia!**
how much   *in*   *biting you*   *I have*   *joy*

se   i 'ni qwo   son
Se   **iniquo**   **son,**
if   *iniquitous*   *I am*

per   ka 'dʒon   'vɔ stra   ɛ   'so lo
per   **cagion**   **vostra**   **è**   **solo.**
through   *cause*   *yours*   *it is*   *only*

ma   in   al 'trwɔ mo   kwi   mi   'kan dʒo
Ma   **in**   **altr'uomo**   **qui**   **mi**   **cangio!**
but   *into*   *other man*   *here*   *myself*   *I change*

kwel   'vɛk: kjo   ma le 'di va mi
Quel   **vecchio**   **maledivami!**
that   *old man*   *cursed me*

tal   pen 'sjɛ ɾo   per 'ke   kon 'tur ba   oɲ: 'ɲor
Tal   **pensiero**   **perchè**   **conturba**   **ognor**
such   *thought*   *why*   *troubles*   *always*

la   'men te   'mi a
la   **mente**   **mia?**
the   *mind*   *mine*

mi   koʎ: ʎe 'ɾa   zven 'tu ɾa
Mi   **coglierà**   **sventura?**
me   *will seize*   *bad luck*

a   nɔ   ɛ   fol: 'li a
Ah   **no!**   **è**   **follia!**
ah   *no*   *it is*   *folly*

LA TRAVIATA

music: Giuseppe Verdi
libretto: Francesco Maria Piave (after the play *La Dame aux Camélias* by Alexandre Dumas fils)

Di Provenza il mar, il suol

di   pro 'vɛn tsa   il   mar   il   swɔl
Di   **Provenza**   **il**   **mar,**   **il**   **suol**
of   *Provence*   *the*   *sea*   *the*   *soil*

ki   dal   kɔr   ti   kan tʃel: 'lɔ
chi   **dal**   **cor**   **ti**   **cancellò?**
who   *from the*   *heart*   *from you*   *erased*

al   na 'ti o   ful 'dʒɛn te   sol
Al   **natio**   **fulgente**   **sol**
from the   *native*   *resplendent*   *sun*

kwal   de 'sti no   ti   fu 'ɾɔ
qual   **destino**   **ti**   **furò?**
what   *destiny*   *you*   *took away*

o   ram: 'men ta   pur   nel   dwɔl
Oh   **rammenta**   **pur**   **nel**   **duol**
oh   *remember*   *yet*   *in the*   *sorrow*

'ki vi   'dʒɔ ja   a   te   bril: 'lɔ
ch'ivi   **gioia**   **a**   **te**   **brillò,**
that there   *joy*   *on*   *you*   *glowed*

e   ke   'pa tʃe   ko 'la   sol
e   che   pace   colà   sol
and   that   peace   there   only

su   te   'splɛn de ɾe   aŋ 'kor   pwɔ
su   te   splendere   ancor   può.
upon   you   to shine   still   is able

'di o   mi   gwi 'dɔ
Dio   mi   guidò!
God   me   guided

a   il   'tu o   'vɛk: kjo   dʒe ni 'tor
Ah,   il   tuo   vecchio   genitor
ah   the   your   old   father

tu   non   'sa i   'kwan to   sof: 'fri
tu   non   sai   quanto   soffrì!
you   not   [you] know   how much   he suffered

te   lon 'ta no   di   sqwal: 'lor
Te   lontano,   di   squallor
you   far away   with   misery

il   'su o   'tet: to   si ko 'pri
il   suo   tetto   si coprì.
the   his   roof   became covered

ma   se   al 'fin   ti   'trɔ vo   aŋ 'kor
Ma   se   alfin   ti   trovo   ancor,
but   if   in the end   you   I find   still

se   in   me   'spɛ me   non   fal: 'li
se   in   me   speme   non   fallì,
if   in   me   hope   not   failed

se   la   'vo tʃe   del: lo 'nor
se   la   voce   dell'onor
if   the   voice   of the honor

in   te   ap: 'pjɛn   non   am: mu 'ti
in   te   appien   non   ammutì,
in   you   fully   not   became silenced

'di o   me za u 'di
Dio   m'esaudì!
God   me has answered

ZAZÀ

music: Ruggero Leoncavallo
libretto: Ruggero Leoncavallo (after the play by Simon and Berton)

Zazà, piccola zingara

dza 'dza   'pik: ko la   'dziŋ ga ɾa
Zazà,   piccola   zingara,
Zazà   little   gypsy

'skja va   dun   'fɔl: le   a 'mo ɾe
schiava   d'un   folle   amore,
slave   of a   foolish   love

tu   non   'sɛ i   'dʒun ta   al   'tɛr mi ne
tu   non   sei   giunta   al   termine
you   not   [you] are   arrived   at the   end

aŋ 'kor del 'tu o do 'lo ɾe
ancor del tuo dolore!
yet of the your grief

'kwan to kon 'vjɛn di 'la gri me
Quanto convien di lagrime
how much it is fitting of tears

ke sul 'tu o 'vol to 'ʃen da
che sul tuo volto scenda
that upon your face should fall

'pri a ke il 'tu o 'so lo e 'du mi le
pria che il tuo solo ed umile
before that the your alone and humble

pelː le gri 'nar ri 'prɛn da
pellegrinar riprenda!
making of a pilgrimage should take up again

tu lo kre 'de sti 'li be ɾo
Tu lo credesti libero;
you him [you] believed free

or la spe 'ran tsa ɛ 'spɛn ta
or la speranza è spenta.
now the hope is extinguished

'o ɾa 'sɛ i tu la 'li be ɾa
Ora sei tu la libera!
now [you] are you the free one

e il 'tu o do 'ver ramː 'men ta
E il tuo dover rammenta...
and the your duty remember

il 'tu o do 'ver
il tuo dover!
the your duty

'a i del soɲː 'ɲa to i 'dilː ljo
Ahi! del sognato idillio
alas of the dreamed-of idyll

'spar ve liŋ 'kan to
sparve l'incanto
disappeared the enchantment

a un 'tratː to
a un tratto!
in a stroke

'u na ma 'ni na 'dan dʒe lo
Una manina d'angelo
a little hand of angel

in dje tredː 'dʒar ta 'fatː to
indietreggiar t'ha fatto!
to draw back you has made

ABOUT THE FRENCH IPA TRANSLITERATIONS
by Martha Gerhart

Following is a table of pronunciation for French lyric diction in singing as transliterated in this volume.

THE VOWELS

symbol	nearest equivalent in English	descriptive notes
[ɑ]	as in "f<u>a</u>ther"	the "dark 'a'"
[a]	in English only in dialect; comparable to the Italian "a"	the "bright 'a'"
[e]	no equivalent in English; as in the German "Schnee"	the "closed 'e'": [i] in the [ɛ] position
[ɛ]	as in "b<u>e</u>t"	the "open 'e'"
[i]	as in "f<u>ee</u>t"	
[o]	no equivalent in English as a pure vowel; approximately as in "<u>o</u>pen"	the "closed 'o'"
[ɔ]	as in "<u>ou</u>ght"	the "open 'o'"
[u]	as in "bl<u>ue</u>"	
[y]	no equivalent in English	[i] sustained with the lips rounded to a [u] position
[ø]	no equivalent in English	[e] sustained with the lips rounded almost to [u]
[œ] *	as in "<u>ea</u>rth" without pronouncing any "r"	[ɛ] with lips in the [ɔ] position
[ɑ̃]	no equivalent in English	the nasal "a": [ɔ] with nasal resonance added
[ɔ̃]	no equivalent in English	the nasal "o": [o] with nasal resonance added
[ɛ̃]	no equivalent in English	the nasal "e": as in English "c<u>a</u>t" with nasal resonance added
[œ̃]	no equivalent in English	the nasal "œ": as in English "<u>uh</u>, h<u>uh</u>" with nasal resonance added

* Some diction manuals transliterate the neutral, unstressed syllables in French as a "schwa" [ə].
Refer to authoritative published sources concerning such sophistications of French lyric diction.

THE SEMI-CONSONANTS

[ɥ]	no equivalent in English	a [y] in the tongue position of [i] and the lip position of [u]
[j]	as in "<u>e</u>we," "<u>y</u>es"	a "glide"
[w]	as in "<u>w</u>e," "<u>w</u>ant"	

THE CONSONANTS

[b]	as in "bad"	with a few exceptions
[c]	[k], as in "cart"	with some exceptions
[ç]	as in "sun"	when initial or medial, before *a*, *o*, or *u*
[d]	usually, as in "door"	becomes [t] in liaison
[f]	usually, as in "foot"	becomes [v] in liaison
[g]	usually, as in "gate"	becomes [k] in liaison; see also [ʒ]
[k]	as in "kite"	
[l]	as in "lift"	with some exceptions
[m]	as in "mint"	with a few exceptions
[n]	as in "nose"	with a few exceptions
[ɲ]	as in "onion"	almost always the pronunciation of the "gn" combination
[p]	as in "pass"	except when silent (final) and in a few rare words
[r] *	no equivalent in English	flipped (or occasionally rolled) "r"
[s]	as in "solo"	with exceptions; becomes [z] in liaison
[t]	as in "tooth"	with some exceptions
[v]	as in "voice"	
[x]	[ks] as in "extra," [gz] as in "exist," [z] as in "Oz," or [s] as in "sent"	becomes [z] in liaison
[z]	as in "zone"	with some exceptions
[ʒ]	as in "rouge"	usually, "g" when initial or mediant before *e*, *i*, or *y*; also, "j" in any position
[ʃ]	as in "shoe"	

* The conversational "uvular 'r'" is used in popular French song and cabaret but is not considered appropriate for singing in the classical repertoire.

LIAISON AND ELISION

Liaison is common in French. It is the sounding (linking) of a normally silent final consonant with the vowel (or mute h) beginning the next word. Its use follows certain rules; apart from the rules, the final choice as to whether or not to make a liaison depends on good taste and/or the advice of experts.

Examples of liaison, with their IPA:

les oiseaux   est ici
le‿ zwa zo   ɛ‿ ti si

Elision is the linking of a consonant followed by a final unstressed *e* with the vowel (or mute *h*) beginning the next word.

examples, with their IPA: elle est   votre âme
ɛ‿ lɛ   vɔ‿ tra mœ

The linking symbol [‿] is given in these transliterations for both **elision** and for (recommended) **liaisons**.

CARMEN

music: Georges Bizet
libretto: Henri Meilhac and Ludovic Halévy (after the novel by Prosper Mérimée)

Votre toast, je peux vous le rendre
(Toreador Song)

vɔ trœ	tost	ʒœ	pø	vu	lœ	rã drœ
Votre	**toast,**	**je**	**peux**	**vous**	**le**	**rendre,**
your	*toast*	*I*	*can*	*to you*	*it*	*return*

se ɲor	ka	ra vɛk	lɛ	sɔl da
Señors,	**car**	**avec**	**les**	**soldats,**
gentlemen	*for*	*with*	*the*	*soldiers*

wi	lɛ	tɔ re ro	pœ vœ	sã tã drœ
oui,	**les**	**toréros**	**peuvent**	**s'entendre:**
yes	*the*	*bullfighters*	*are able*	*to agree*

pur	plɛ zir	il	zɔ̃	le	kɔ̃ ba
pour	**plaisirs,**	**ils**	**ont**	**les**	**combats!**
for	*pleasures*	*they*	*have*	*the*	*combats*

lœ	sir	kɛ	plɛ̃	sɛ	ʒur	dœ	fe tœ
Le	**cirque**	**est**	**plein;**	**c'est**	**jour**	**de**	**fête!**
the	*arena*	*is*	*full*	*it is*	*day*	*of*	*festival*

lœ	sir	kɛ	plɛ̃	dy	o	tã ba
Le	**cirque**	**est**	**plein**	**du**	**haut en**	**bas.**
the	*arena*	*is*	*full*	*from the*	*top to*	*bottom*

le	spɛk ta tœr	per dã	la	tɛ tœ
Les	**spectateurs,**	**perdant**	**la**	**tête,**
the	*spectators*	*losing*	*the*	*head*

sɛ̃ ter pɛ lœ	a	grã	fra kɑ
s'interpellent	**à**	**grand**	**fracas!**
heckle each other	*at*	*great*	*noise*

a pɔ strɔ fœ	kri	ze	ta pa ʒœ
Apostrophes,	**cris,**	**et**	**tapage**
reproaches	*cries*	*and*	*uproar*

pu se	ʒy skœ za	la	fy rœr
poussés	**jusques à**	**la**	**fureur!**
pushed	*as far as to*	*the*	*fury*

kar	sɛ	la	fɛ tœ	dy	ku ra ʒœ
Car	**c'est**	**la**	**fête**	**du**	**courage!**
for	*it is*	*the*	*celebration*	*of the*	*courage*

sɛ	la	fɛ tœ	de	ʒã	dœ kœr
C'est	**la**	**fête**	**des**	**gens**	**de cœur!**
it is	*the*	*celebration*	*of the*	*people*	*of good heart*

a lɔ̃	ã	gar dœ	a
Allons!	**en**	**garde!**	**Ah!**
let's go	*on*	*garde*	*ah*

tɔ re a dor	ã	gar dœ
Toréador,	**en**	**garde!**
Toreador	*on*	*garde*

e	sɔ̃ ʒœ	bjɛ̃	wi
Et	**songe**	**bien,**	**oui,**
and	*think of*	*well*	*yes*

34

só	ʒã	kõ ba tã
songe	**en**	**combattant**
think of	*while*	*fighting*

kœ̃	nœj	nwar	tœ	rœ gar
qu'un	**œil**	**noir**	**te**	**regarde**
that an	*eye*	*dark*	*you*	*watches*

de	kœ	la mur	ta tã
et	**que**	**l'amour**	**t'attend!**
and	*that*	*the love*	*you awaits*

Note: if a breath is taken after "te regarde": tœ rœ gard /et kœ...

tɔ re a dor	la mur	ta tã
Toréador,	**l'amour**	**t'attend!**
Toreador	*the love*	*you awaits*

tu	dœ̃	ku	õ	fɛ	si lã sœ
Tout	**d'un**	**coup**	**on**	**fait**	**silence.**
all	*in a*	*flash*	*one*	*makes*	*silence*

a	kœ	sœ pɑ sœ til
Ah!	**que**	**se passe-t-il?**
ah	*what*	*is happening*

ply	dœ	kri	sɛ	lɛ̃ stã
Plus	**de**	**cris,**	**c'est**	**l'instant!**
more	*of*	*cries*	*it is*	*the moment*

lœ	tɔ ro	se lã
Le	**taureau**	**s'élance**
the	*bull*	*rears*

sã	bõ di sã	ɔr dy	tɔ ril
en	**bondissant**	**hors du**	**toril!**
in	*bounding*	*out of the*	*pen*

il	se lã sœ	i	lã	tril	fra pœ
Il	**s'élance!**	**il**	**entre,**	**il**	**frappe!**
he	*rears*	*he*	*enters*	*he*	*strikes*

œ̃	ʃœ val	ru lœ	ã trɛ nã	tœ̃	pi ka dɔr
Un	**cheval**	**roule,**	**entraînant**	**un**	**picador.**
a	*horse*	*rolls over*	*dragging*	*a*	*picador*

a	bra vo	tɔ ro	yr lœ	la	fu lœ
« Ah!	**Bravo!**	**Toro! »**	**hurle**	**la**	**foule!**
ah	*well done*	*bull*	*roars*	*the*	*crowd*

lœ	tɔ ro	va	il	vjɛ̃	e	fra	pã kɔr
Le	**taureau**	**va,**	**il**	**vient,**	**et**	**frappe**	**encor!**
the	*bull*	*goes*	*he*	*comes*	*and*	*strikes*	*again*

ã	sœ ku ã	sɛ	bã dœ ri jœ
En	**secouant**	**ses**	**banderilles,**
in	*shaking*	*his*	*banderillas*

plɛ̃	dœ	fy rœr	il	kur
plein	**de**	**fureur,**	**il**	**court!**
full	*of*	*fury*	*he*	*runs*

lœ	sir	kɛ	plɛ̃	dœ	sã
Le	**cirque**	**est**	**plein**	**de**	**sang!**
the	*arena*	*is*	*full*	*of*	*blood*

ɔ   sœ sov
On   **se sauve,**
one   *hurries away*

ɔ̃   frã ʃi   lɛ   gri jœ
on   **franchit**   **les**   **grilles!**
one   *jumps over*   *the*   *railings*

sɛ   tɔ̃   tur   mɛ̃ tœ nã
C'est   **ton**   **tour**   **maintenant!**
it is   *your*   *turn*   *now*

a lɔ̃   ã   gar dœ   a
Allons!   **en**   **garde!**   **Ah!**
let's go   *on*   *garde*   *ah*

FAUST

music: Charles Gounod

libretto: Jules Barbier and Michel Carré (after the drama by Johann Wolfgang von Goethe)

Avant de quitter ces lieux

o   sɛ̃ tœ   me da jœ
Ô   **sainte**   **médaille,**
o   *sacred*   *medallion*

ki   mœ   vjɛ̃   dœ   ma   sœr
qui   **me**   **viens**   **de**   **ma**   **sœur—**
which   *to me*   *comes*   *from*   *my*   *sister*

o   ʒur   dœ   la   ba tɑ jœ
au   **jour**   **de**   **la**   **bataille,**
on the   *day*   *of*   *the*   *battle*

pu‿   re kar te   la   mɔr
pour   **écarter**   **la**   **mort,**
for   *to keep away*   *the*   *death*

rɛ stœ   la   syr   mɔ̃   kœr
reste   **là**   **sur**   **mon**   **cœur!**
remain   *there*   *upon*   *my*   *heart*

a vã   dœ   ki te   sɛ   ljø
Avant   **de**   **quitter**   **ces**   **lieux,**
before   *of*   *to leave*   *these*   *premises*

sɔl   na tal   dœ   mɛ‿   za jø
sol   **natal**   **de**   **mes**   **aïeux,**
soil   *native*   *of*   *my*   *ancestors*

a   twa   sɛ ɲœ‿   re   rwa   dɛ   sjø
à   **toi,**   **Seigneur**   **et**   **Roi**   **des**   **cieux,**
to   *you*   *Lord*   *and*   *King*   *of the*   *heavens*

ma   sœr   ʒœ   kɔ̃ fi œ
ma   **sœur**   **je**   **confie.**
my   *sister*   *I*   *entrust*

dɛ ɲœ   dœ   tu   dã ʒe
Daigne   **de**   **tout**   **danger**
deign   *from*   *all*   *danger*

tu ʒur   la   prɔ te ʒe
toujours   **la**   **protéger—**
always   *her*   *to protect*

sɛ tœ   sœr   si   ʃe ri œ
cette   **sœur**   **si**   **chérie.**
this   *sister*   *so*   *dearly loved*

dɛ ɲœ   dœ   tu   dɑ̃ ʒe   la   prɔ te ʒe
Daigne   **de**   **tout**   **danger**   **la**   **protéger.**
deign   *from*   *all*   *danger*   *her*   *to protect*

de li vre   dy nœ   tri stœ   pɑ̃ se œ
Délivré   **d'une**   **triste**   **pensée,**
freed   *from a*   *sad*   *thought*

ʒi re   ʃɛr ʃe   la   glwa rœ
j'irai   **chercher**   **la**   **gloire**
I shall go   *to seek*   *the*   *glory*

la   glwa‿ro   sɛ̃   dɛ‿   zɛ nœ mi
la   **gloire**   **au**   **sein**   **des**   **ennemis.**
the   *glory*   *in the*   *lap*   *of the*   *enemies*

lœ   prœ mje   lœ   ply   bra‿
Le   **premier,**   **le**   **plus**   **brave**
the   *first*   *the*   *most*   *brave*

vo   fɔr   dœ   la   mɛ le ə
au   **fort**   **de**   **la**   **mêlée,**
in the   *thick*   *of*   *the*   *conflict*

ʒi re   kɔ̃ ba trœ   pur   mɔ̃   pɛ i
j'irai   **combattre**   **pour**   **mon**   **pays.**
I will go   *to fight*   *for*   *my*   *country*

e   si   vɛr   lɥi   djø   mœ   ra pɛ lœ
Et   **si,**   **vers**   **lui,**   **Dieu**   **me**   **rappelle,**
and   *if*   *to*   *him*   *God*   *me*   *calls*

ʒœ   vɛ jœ re   syr   twa   fi dɛ lœ
je   **veillerai**   **sur**   **toi**   **fidèle,**
I   *shall watch*   *over*   *you*   *faithful*

o   mar gœ ri tœ
ô   **Marguerite!**
o   *Marguerite*

o   rwa   dɛ   sjø
Ô   **Roi**   **des**   **cieux,**
o   *King*   *of the*   *heavens*

ʒɛ tœ   lɛ‿   zjø
jette   **les**   **yeux—**
cast   *the*   *eyes*

prɔ tɛ ʒœ   mar gœ ri tœ
protège   **Marguerite,**
protect   *Marguerite*

rwa   dɛ   sjø
Roi   **des**   **cieux!**
King   *of the*   *heavens*

HAMLET

music: Ambroise Thomas
libretto: Jules Barbier and Michel Carré (after the tragedy by William Shakespeare)

Ô vin, dissipe la tristesse

o	vɛ̃	di si pœ	la	tri stɛ sœ
Ô	**vin,**	**dissipe**	**la**	**tristesse**
o	*wine*	*dissipate*	*the*	*sadness*

ki	pɛ zœ	syr	mɔ̃	kœr
qui	**pèse**	**sur**	**mon**	**cœur!**
which	*weighs*	*on*	*my*	*heart*

a	mwa	lɛ	rɛ vœ	dœ	li vrɛ sœ
À	**moi**	**les**	**rêves**	**de**	**l'ivresse**
to	*me*	*the*	*dreams*	*from*	*the intoxication*

e	lœ	ri rœ	mɔ kœr
et	**le**	**rire**	**moqueur!**
and	*the*	*laughter*	*mocking*

o	li kœ‿	rɑ̃ ʃɑ̃ tœ rɛ sœ
Ô	**liqueur**	**enchanteresse,**
o	*liquor*	*enchanting*

vɛr sœ	li vrɛ‿
verse	**l'ivresse**
pour	*the intoxication*

se	lu bli	dɑ̃	mɔ̃	kœr
et	**l'oubli**	**dans**	**mon**	**cœur!**
and	*the oblivion*	*into*	*my*	*heart*

du sœ	li kœr
Douce	**liqueur!**
sweet	*liquor*

la	vi	ɛ	sɔ̃ brœ
La	**vie**	**est**	**sombre;**
the	*life*	*is*	*gloomy*

lɛ‿	zɑ̃	sɔ̃	kur
les	**ans**	**sont**	**courts.**
the	*years*	*are*	*short*

dœ	no	bo	ʒur
De	**nos**	**beaux**	**jours**
of	*our*	*beautiful*	*days*

djø	sɛ	lœ	nɔ̃ brœ
Dieu	**sait**	**le**	**nombre.**
God	*knows*	*the*	*number*

ʃa kœ̃	e lɑs	pɔr‿	ti si bɑ
Chacun,	**hélas!**	**porte**	**ici-bas**
each one	*alas*	*bears*	*here below*

sa	lur dœ	ʃɛ nœ
sa	**lourde**	**chaîne—**
his	*heavy*	*chain*

kry ɛl	dœ vwar
cruels	**devoirs,**
cruel	*obligations*

lɔ̃   de zɛ spwar   dœ   lɑ‿   my mɛ nœ
longs   désespoirs   de   l'âme   humaine!
long   desperations   of   the soul   human

lwɛ̃   dœ   nu   nwar   pre za ʒœ
Loin   de   nous,   noirs   présages!
far   from   us   dark   forebodings

lɛ   ply   sa ʒœ   sɔ̃   lɛ   fu
Les   plus   sages   sont   les   fous!
the   most   wise   are   the   fools

a
Ah!
ah

lœ   vɛ̃   di si pœ   la   tri stɛ sœ
Le   vin   dissipe   la   tristesse
the   wine   dissipates   the   sadness

ki   pɛ zœ   syr   mɔ̃   kœr
qui   pèse   sur   mon   cœur!
which   weighs   on   my   heart

vɛr sœ nu   li vrɛ sœ
Verse-nous   l'ivresse!
pour on us   the intoxication

HÉRODIADE

music: Jules Massenet
libretto: Paul Milliet, "Henri Grémont," a pseudonym for Georges Hartmann, and Angelo Zanardini (after the story by Gustave Flaubert)

Vision fugitive

sœ   brœ va ʒœ   pu rɛ   mœ   dɔ ne‿   rœ̃   tɛl   re vœ
Ce   breuvage   pourrait   me   donner   un   tel   rêve!
this   potion   should be able   to me   to give   a   such   dream

ʒœ   pu rɛ   la   rœ vwar
Je   pourrais   la   revoir...
I   should be able   her   to see again

kɔ̃ tɑ̃ ple   sa   bo te
contempler   sa   beauté!
to contemplate   her   beauty

di vi nœ   vɔ lyp te   a   mɛ   rœ gar   prɔ mi zœ
Divine   volupté   à   mes   regards   promise!
divine   voluptuousness   to   my   gazes   promised

ɛ spe rɑ̃ sœ   tro   brɛ vœ
Espérance   trop   brève
hope   too   brief

ki   vjɛ̃   bɛr se   mɔ̃   kœr
qui   viens   bercer   mon   cœur
which   comes   to lull   my   heart

e   tru ble   ma   rɛ zɔ̃
et   troubler   ma   raison...
and   to trouble   my   reason

a nœ tɑ̃ fɥi pɑ du‿ si ly zi ɔ̃
Ah! ne t'enfuis pas, douce illusion!
ah not fly away [not] sweet illusion

vi zi ɔ̃ fy ʒi ti‿ ve tu ʒur pur sɥi vi œ
Vision fugitive et toujours poursuivie—
vision fleeting and always pursued

ɑ̃ ʒœ mi ste ri ø ki prɑ̃
ange mystérieux qui prends
angel mysterious who takes over

tu tœ ma vi œ
toute ma vie...
all my life

a sɛ twa kœ ʒœ vø vwa‿
Ah! c'est toi que je veux voir,
ah it is you that I wish to see

ro mɔ̃‿ na mur o mɔ̃‿ nɛ spwar
ô mon amour! ô mon espoir!
oh my love oh my hope

vi zi ɔ̃ fy ʒi ti vœ sɛ twa
Vision fugitive, c'est toi
vision fleeting it is you

ki prɑ̃ tu tœ ma vi œ
qui prends toute ma vie.
who take over all my life

tœ prɛ se dɑ̃ mɛ bra
Te presser dans mes bras!
you to press in my arms

sɑ̃ tir ba trœ tɔ̃ kœr
Sentir battre ton cœur
to feel to beat your heart

dy‿ na mu rœ‿ zar dœr
d'une amoureuse ardeur!
with a loving ardor

pɥi mu ri‿ rɑ̃ la se
Puis, mourir enlacés
then to die entwined

dɑ̃‿ zy nœ mɛ‿ mi vrɛ sœ
dans une même ivresse—
in a same intoxication

pur sɛ trɑ̃ spɔr
pour ces transports,
for those raptures

pur sɛ tœ flɑ mœ
pour cette flamme,
for that passion

a sɑ̃ rɛ mɔ‿ re sɑ̃ plɛ̃ tœ
ah! sans remords et sans plainte
ah without remorse and without complaint

ʒœ   dɔ nœ rɛ   mɔ̃   na mœ   pur   twa
je   donnerais   mon   âme   pour   toi,
I   would give   my   soul   for   you

mɔ̃   na mur   mɔ̃   nɛ spwar
mon   amour,   mon   espoir!
my   love   my   hope

wi   sɛ   twa   mɔ̃   na mur
Oui!   c'est   toi!   mon   amour!
yes   it is   you   my   love

twa   mɔ̃   sœ   la mur   mɔ̃   nɛ spwar
Toi,   mon   seul   amour,   mon   espoir!
you   my   only   love   my   hope

ROMÉO ET JULIETTE

music: Charles Gounod
libretto: Jules Barbier and Michel Carré (after the tragedy by William Shakespeare)

Mab, la reine des mensonges
(Ballad of Queen Mab)

mab   la   rɛ nœ   dɛ   mɑ̃ sɔ̃ ʒœ
Mab,   la   reine   des   mensonges,
Mab   the   queen   of the   delusions

pre zi   do   sɔ̃ ʒœ
préside   aux   songes.
presides   over the   dreams

ply   le ʒɛ rœ   kœ   lœ   vɑ̃   de sœ vɑ̃
Plus   légère   que   le   vent   décevant,
more   light   than   the   wind   deceptive

a tra vɛr   lɛ spa sœ
à travers   l'espace,
through   the space

a tra vɛr   la   nɥi
à travers   la   nuit,
through   the   night

ɛ lœ   pɑ sœ   ɛ lœ   fɥi
elle   passe,   elle   fuit!
she   passes   she   flies

sɔ̃   ʃɑr   kœ   la to mœ   ra pi
Son   char,   que   l'atome   rapide
her   chariot   which   the mite   swift

dɑ̃ trɛ nœ   dɑ̃   le tɛr   lɛ̃ pi dœ
entraîne   dans   l'éther   limpide,
draws   through   the ether   limpid

fy   fɛ   dy nœ   nwa zɛ tœ   vi dœ
fut   fait   d'une   noisette   vide
was   made   from a   hazel nut   hollow

par   vɛr dœ tɛ rœ   lœ   ʃa rɔ̃
par   ver de terre   le   charron!
by   earthworm   the   wheelright

lɛ	ar nɛ	syp ti lœ	dã tɛ‿
Les	**harnais,**	**subtile**	**dentelle,**
the	*harnesses*	*delicate*	*lace*

lɔ̃‿	te te	de ku pe	dã	lɛ lœ
ont	**été**	**découpés**	**dans**	**l'aile**
have	*been*	*cut out*	*out of*	*the wing*

dœ	kɛl kœ	ver tœ	so tœ rɛ lœ
de	**quelque**	**verte**	**sauterelle**
of	*some*	*green*	*grasshopper*

par	sɔ̃	kɔ ʃe	lœ	mu ʃœ rɔ̃
par	**son**	**cocher,**	**le**	**moucheron!**
by	*her*	*coachman*	*the*	*gnat*

œ̃‿	nɔs	dœ	gri jɔ̃	sɛr	dœ	mã‿
Un	**os**	**de**	**grillon**	**sert**	**de**	**manche**
a	*bone*	*of*	*cricket*	*serves*	*as*	*handle*

ʃa	sɔ̃	fwɛ	dɔ̃	la	mɛ ʃœ	blã‿
à	**son**	**fouet,**	**dont**	**la**	**mèche**	**blanche**
for	*his*	*whip*	*of which*	*the*	*lash*	*white*

ʃɛ	pri‿	zo	rɛ jɔ̃	ki	se pã ʃœ
est	**prise**	**au**	**rayon**	**qui**	**s'épanche**
is	*taken*	*from the*	*ray of light*	*which*	*pours out*

dœ	fe be	ra sã blã	sa	kur
de	**Phoebé**	**rassemblant**	**sa**	**cour.**
from	*Phoebus*	*assembling*	*his*	*court*

ʃa kœ	nɥi	dã	sɛ‿	te ki pa ʒɛ
Chaque	**nuit,**	**dans**	**cet**	**équipage,**
each	*night*	*in*	*that*	*carriage*

mab	vi zi tœ	syr	sɔ̃	pɑ sa ʒœ
Mab	**visite,**	**sur**	**son**	**passage,**
Mab	*visits*	*along*	*her*	*way*

le pu	ki	rɛ vœ	dœ	vœ vaʒ
l'époux	**qui**	**rêve**	**de**	**veuvage**
the husband	*who*	*dreams*	*of*	*widowerhood*

e	la mã	ki	rɛ vœ	da mur
et	**l'amant**	**qui**	**rêve**	**d'amour!**
and	*the lover*	*who*	*dreams*	*of love*

a	sɔ̃‿	na prɔ ʃœ	la	kɔ kɛ tœ
À	**son**	**approche,**	**la**	**coquette**
at	*her*	*approach*	*the*	*coquette*

rɛ vœ	da tur‿	ze	dœ	twa lɛ tœ
rêve	**d'atours**	**et**	**de**	**toilette,**
dreams	*of finery*	*and*	*of*	*dressing up*

lœ	kur ti zã	fɛ	la	kur bɛ tœ
le	**courtisan**	**fait**	**la**	**courbette,**
the	*courtier*	*makes*	*the*	*stooping bow*

lœ	pɔ ɛ tœ	ri mœ	sɛ	vɛr
le	**poête**	**rime**	**ses**	**vers!**
the	*poet*	*rhymes*	*his*	*verses*

42

a la va‿ rã sõ ʒi tœ sõ brœ
À l'avare en son gîte sombre
to the miser in his lodgings gloomy

ɛ‿ lu vrœ dɛ tre zɔr sã nõ bre
elle ouvre des trésors sans nombre,
she opens of treasures without number

e la li bɛr te ri dã lõ brœ
et la liberté rit dans l'ombre
and the liberty smiles in the darkness

o pri sɔ nje ʃar ʒe dœ fɛr
au prisonnier chargé de fers.
at the prisoner charged with fetters

lœ sɔl da rɛ vœ dã by ska dœ
Le soldat rêve d'embuscades,
the soldier dreams of ambushes

dœ ba tɑ jœ e de stɔ ka dœ
de batailles et d'estocades;
of battles and of thrusts

ɛ lœ lɥi vɛr sœ lɛ rɑ za dœ
elle lui verse les rasades
she for him pours the brimfull glasses

dõ sɛ lɔ rje sõ‿ ta ro ze
dont ses lauriers sont arrosés.
with which his laurels are bathed

e twa kœ̃ su pi‿ re fa ru ʃœ
Et toi, qu'un soupir effarouche
and you whom a sigh startles

kã ty rœ po zœ syr ta ku ʃœ
quand tu reposes sur ta couche,
when you rest on your bed

o vjɛrʒ ɛ‿ le flœ rœ ta bu ʃœ
ô vierge! elle effleure ta bouche
oh maiden she grazes your mouth

e tœ fɛ rɛ ve dœ be ze
et te fait rêver de baisers!
and you makes to dream of kisses

THAÏS

music: Jules Massenet
libretto: Louis Gallet (after the novel by Anatole France)

Voilà donc la terrible cité

vwa la   dɔ̃   la   tɛ ri blœ   si te
Voilà   **donc**   **la**   **terrible**   **cité!**
there is   *hence*   *the*   *terrible*   *city*

a lɛk sɑ̃ dri œ   u   ʒœ   sɥi ne
Alexandrie!   **où**   **je**   **suis né**
Alexandria   *where*   *I*   *was born*

dɑ̃   lœ   pe ʃe
dans   **le**   **péché—**
in   *the*   *sin*

lɛr   bri jɑ̃   u   ʒe   rɛ spi re
l'air   **brillant**   **où**   **j'ai**   **respiré**
the air   *sparkling*   *where*   *I have*   *breathed*

la frø   par fœ̃   dœ   la   lyk syr œ
l'affreux   **parfum**   **de**   **la**   **luxure!**
the hideous   *scent*   *of*   *the*   *lust*

vwa la   la   mɛr   vɔ lyp ty œ zœ
Voilà   **la**   **mer**   **voluptueuse**
there is   *the*   *sea*   *voluptuous*

u   ʒe ku tɛ   ʃɑ̃ te
où   **j'écoutais**   **chanter**
where   *I listened to*   *[to] sing*

la   si rɛ   no   zjø   dɔr
la   **sirène**   **aux**   **yeux**   **d'or!**
the   *siren*   *with the*   *eyes*   *of gold*

wi   vwa la   mɔ̃   bɛr so
Oui,   **voilà**   **mon**   **berceau**
yes   *there is*   *my*   *cradle*

sœ lɔ̃   la   ʃɛr
selon   **la**   **chair,**
according to   *the*   *flesh*

a lɛk sɑ̃ dri œ   o   ma   pa tri œ
Alexandrie!   **Ô**   **ma**   **patrie!**
Alexandria   *oh*   *my*   *native land*

mɔ̃   bɛr so   ma   pa tri œ
Mon   **berceau,**   **ma**   **patrie!**
my   *cradle*   *my*   *native land*

dœ   tɔ̃   na mur
De   **ton**   **amour**
from   *your*   *love*

ʒe   de tur ne   mɔ̃   kœr
j'ai   **détourné**   **mon**   **cœur.**
I have   *turned away*   *my*   *heart*

pur   ta   ri ʃɛ sœ
Pour   **ta**   **richesse**
for   *your*   *riches*

44

ʒœ tœ ɛ
je te hais!
I you hate

pur ta si ɑ̃‿ se ta bo te
Pour ta science et ta beauté,
for your knowledge and your beauty

ʒœ tœ ɛ
je te hais!
I you hate

e mɛ̃ tœ nɑ̃ ʒœ tœ mo di
Et maintenant je te maudis
and now I you curse

kɔ‿ mœ̃ tɑ̃ plœ ɑ̃ te
comme un temple hanté
as a temple haunted

par lɛ‿ zɛ pri‿ zɛ̃ pyr
par les esprits impurs!
by the spirits unclean

vœ ne ɑ̃ ʒœ dy sjɛl
Venez! anges du ciel!
come angels of the heaven

su flœ dœ djø
souffles de Dieu!
breaths from God

par fy me dy ba tœ mɑ̃ dœ vo‿ zɛ lœ
Parfumez, du battement de vos ailes,
scent by the flapping of your wings

lɛr kɔ rɔ̃ py ki va mɑ̃ vi rɔ ne
l'air corrompu qui va m'environner!
the air corrupt which is going me to surround

ABOUT THE GERMAN IPA TRANSLITERATIONS
by Irene Spiegelman

TRANSLATIONS

As every singer has experienced, word-by-word translations are usually awkward, often not understandable, especially in German where the verb usually is split up with one part in second position of the main clause and the rest at the end of the sentence. Sometimes it is a second verb, sometimes it is a little word that looks like a preposition. Since prepositions never come by themselves, these are usually *separable prefixes to the verb*. In order to look up the meaning of the verb this prefix has to be reunited with the verb in order to find the correct meaning in the dictionary. They cannot be looked up by themselves. Therefore, in the word-by-word translation they are marked with ¹) and do not show any words.

Note: In verbs with separable prefixes, the prefix gets the emphasis. If a separable prefix appears at the end of the sentence, it still needs to be stressed and since many of them start with vowels they even might be glottaled for emphasis.

Also, there are many *reflexive verbs* in German that are not reflexive in English, also the reflexive version of a verb in German often means something very different than the meaning found if the verb is looked up by itself. Reflexive pronouns that are grammatically necessary but do not have a meaning by themselves do not show a translation underneath. They are marked with ²).

Another difference in the use of English and German is that German is using the Present Perfect Tense of the verb where English prefers the use of the Simple Past of the verb. In cases like that, the translation appears under the conjugated part of the verb and none underneath the past participle of the verb at the end of the sentence. Those cases are marked with ³).

One last note concerning the translations: English uses possessive pronouns much more often then German does. So der/die/das in German have at appropriate points been translated as my/your/his.

PRONUNCIATION (EXTENDED IPA SYMBOLS)

The IPA symbols that have been used for the German arias are basically those used in Langenscheidt dictionaries. Other publications have refined some symbols, but after working with young singers for a long time, I find that they usually don't remember which is which sign when the ones for long closed vowels (a and ɑ, or ʏ and y) are too close, and especially with the signs for the open and closed u-umlauts they usually cannot tell which they handwrote into their scores. To make sure that a vowel should be closed there is ":" behind the symbol, i.e. [byːp laɪn]

After having been encouraged to sing on a vowel as long as possible, often the consonants are cut too short. The rule is, "**Vowels can be used to make your voice shine, consonants will help your interpretation!**" This is very often is totally neglected in favor of long vowels, even when the vowels are supposed to be short. Therefore, double consonants show up here in the IPA line. This suggests that they should at least not be neglected. There are voiced consonants on which it is easy to sing (l, m, n) and often give the text an additional dimension. That is not true for explosive consonants (d, t, k), but they open the vowels right in front of them. So the double consonants in these words serve here as reminders. German does not require to double the consonants the way Italian does, but that Italian technique might help to move more quickly to the consonant, and therefore open the vowel or at least don't stretch it, which sometimes turns it into a word with a different meaning altogether.

One idea that is heard over and over again is: "There is no legato in German." The suggestions that are marked here with ⇨ in the IPA line show that **that is not true.** Always elided can be words ending in a vowel with the next word beginning with a vowel. Words that end with a -t sound can be combined with the next word that starts with a t- or a d-. A word ending in -n can be connected to the following beginning -n. But words ending in consonants can also be elided with the next word starting with a vowel. (example: Dann [dan⇨n] könnt' [kœn⇨n⇨] ich [⇨tɪç] mit [mɪt] Fürsten ['fʏr stən] mich ['mɛs⇨sən]). In this example, the arrow symbol suggests to use the double consonant, but also that the end-t in "könnt'" could be used at the beginning of "ich" which makes the word "ich" much less important (which it usually is in German), and could help to shape the words "Fürsten" und "messen" with more importance.

Within the IPA line, sometimes the "⇨" symbol is only at the end of a word and means that combining this word with the next is absolutely possible if it helps the interpretation of the text or the singer does not want to interrupt the beauty of the musical line. The same fact is true if the "⇨" symbol appears within a word and suggests combining syllables. (Since English syllables are viewed differently than German syllables, the IPA line is broken down into German syllables with suggestions for vocal combinations.) The only consonant that should not be combined with the next word is "r," because there are too many combinations that form new words (example: der Eine, the one and only, should not become [de: raɪ nə], the pure one).

One last remark about pronunciation that seems to have become an issue in the last few years: How does one pronounce the a-umlaut = ä. Some singers have been told in their diction classes that ä is pronounced like a closed e. That may be the case in casual language and can be heard on German television. But when the texts that we are dealing with were written the sound was either a long or short open e sound ['mɛ: tçən, ʃpɛːt, 'hɛl tə].

Considering the language, how does one make one's voice shine and still use the text for a sensible interpretation? Look for the words within a phrase that are important to you as the interpreter, as the person who believes what he/she is conveying. In those words use the consonants as extensively as possible. [zzze: llə] and [llli: bə] are usually more expressive than [ze: lə] and [li: bə] , also glottal the beginning vowels. Use the surrounding words for singing legato and show off the voice.

The IPA line not only shows correct pronunciation but is also giving guidelines for interpretation. For instance, R's may be rolled or flipped, or words may be connected or separated at any time as long as they help you with your feeling for the drama of the text. But you are the person who has to decide! Be discriminating! Know what you want to say! Your language will fit with the music perfectly.

THE "R" IN GERMAN DICTION

When most Germans speak an "r" in front of a vowel, it is a sound produced between the far back of the tongue and the uvula, almost like a gargling sound. The r's at the end of syllables take on different sounds and often have a vowel-like quality.

In classical singing, the practice is to use "Italian r's". Since trilling the r at the tip of the tongue seems to be easy for most singers, many texts are rendered with any overdone r's, which are remotely possible. As a result, the r's take over the whole text and diminish the meaning and phrasing of the sentences. By being discriminating in using rolled r's in an opera text, the phrasing, i.e. interpretation, as well as the chance of understanding the sung text can be improved.

Essentially, there are three categories of words with different suggestions about the use of r's:

ALWAYS ROLL THE R	END-R'S IN SHORT ONE-SYLLABLE WORDS	END-R'S IN PREFIXES AND SUFFIXES
a) before vowels: Rose ['ro: zə] tragen ['tra: gən] sprechen ['ʃprɛ: xən] Trug [tru:k] führen ['fy: rən] b) after vowels in the main syllable of the word: bergen ['bɛr gən] Herz [hɛrts] Schwert [ʃve:rt] durch [dʊrç] geworben [gə 'vɔr bən] hart [hart]	End-r's in short one-syllable words that have a closed vowel can be replaced with a short a-vowel, marked in the IPA line with ᵃ. der [de:ᵃ] er [e:ᵃ] wir [vi:ᵃ] hier [hi:ᵃ] vor [fo:ᵃ] nur [nu:ᵃ] **Note:** **After an a-vowel a replacement of r by ᵃ would not sound. Therefore end-r's after any a should be rolled.** **war [va:r]** **gar [ga:r]**	Prefixes: ver- er- zer- Here, e and r could be pronounced as a schwa-sound, almost like a short open e combined with a very short ᵃ. If desired, the r could also be flipped with one little flip in order not to overpower the main part of the word which is coming up. In the IPA-line this is marked with ʀ. verbergen [fɛʀ 'bɛr gən] erklären [ɛʀ 'klɛ: rən] Suffix: -er These suffixes are most of the time not important for the interpretation of the text. Therefore, the schwa-sound as explained above works in most cases very well. It is marked in the IPA-line with ɚ. e-Suffixes are marked with ə. guter ['gu: tɚ] gute ['gu: tə] Winter ['vɪn tɚ] Meistersinger ['maɪ stɚ sɪ ŋɚ] (compound noun, both parts end in -er)

HÄNSEL UND GRETEL

music: Engelbert Humperdinck
libretto: Adelheid Wette (after a story by the brothers Grimm)

Ach, wir armen Leute

'ral la la 'la	'ral la la 'la			
Rallalala,	**rallalala!**			
Tralalala,	*tralalala!*			

'haɪ sa	'mʊt tɚ	ɪç	bɪn	daː
Heißa	**Mutter,**	**ich**	**bin**	**da!**
(Be) happy	*mother,*	*I*	*am*	*here!*

'brɪ ŋə	'glʏk⇨	ʊnt	'gloː ria
Bringe	**Glück**	**und**	**Gloria!**
Bring	*happiness*	*and*	*glory!*

ax	viːᵃ	'ar mən	'ar mən	'lɔy tə
Ach,	**wir**	**armen,**	**armen**	**Leute—**
Ah,	*we*	*poor,*	*poor*	*people—*

'al lə	'taː gə	zoː	viː	'hɔy tə
alle	**Tage**	**so**	**wie**	**heute:**
every	*day*	*just*	*like*	*today:*

ɪn	deːm	'bɔy təl	aɪn	'groː səs	'lɔx
in	**dem**	**Beutel**	**ein**	**großes**	**Loch,**
in	*the*	*purse*	*a*	*big*	*hole,*

ʊnt⇨	ɪm	'maː gən	aɪn	'grøː⇨ srəs	nɔx
und	**im**	**Magen**	**ein**	**größ'res**	**noch.**
and	*in the*	*stomach*	*a*	*bigger one,*	*still.*

hʊ ŋɚ	ɪst⇨	deːᵃ	bɛs tə	kɔx
Hunger	**ist**	**der**	**beste**	**Koch!**
Hunger	*is*	*the*	*best*	*cook!*

jaː	iːᵃ	'raɪ çən	kœn⇨	⇨tɔyç	'laː bən
Ja,	**ihr**	**Reichen**	**könnt**	**euch**	**laben;**
Yes,	*you*	*rich people*	*can*	*2)*	*feast;*

'viːᵃ	diː	'nɪçts	tzuː	'ɛs sən	'haː bən
wir,	**die**	**nichts**	**zu**	**essen**	**haben**
we,	*who*	*nothing*	*to*	*eat*	*have*

'naː gən	ax	diː	'gan tsə	vɔx
nagen,	**ach,**	**die**	**ganze**	**Woch',**
nibble,	*ah,*	*the*	*whole*	*week,*

'ziː bən	'taːk	an	'aɪ nəm	'knɔx
sieben	**Tag'**	**an**	**einem**	**Knoch'!**
seven	*days*	*on*	*one*	*bone!*

ax　vi:ᵃ　zɪnt　ja:　　　'gɛrn　　zu: 'fri: dən
Ach,　wir　sind　ja　　　gern　　zufrieden,
Ah,　we　are　after all　happily　content,

dɛn　das　'glʏk⇨　ɪs⇨　⇨tso:　fɛʀ 'ʃi: dən
denn　das　Glück　ist　so　verschieden!
for　the　good luck　is　very　different!

a: bɚ　'va:r　ɪsts⇨　dɔx
Aber　wahr　ist's　doch,
But　true　is it　nevertheless,

'a:r mu:t　ist⇨　aɪn　'ʃve: rəs　jɔx
Armut　ist　ein　schweres　Joch!
poverty　is　a　heavy　burden!

ja: ja:　de:ᵃ　hʊ ŋɚ　kɔx⇨　tʃo:n　'gu:t
Ja ja,　der　Hunger　kocht　schon　gut,
Oh yes,　(the)　hunger　cooks　really　well,

zo: 'fɛrn　e:ᵃ　kɔm⇨man di: rən　tu:t
sofern　er　kommandieren　tut;
if　it　the commanding　does;

al⇨laɪn　vas　nʏtst⇨　de:ᵃ　kɔm⇨man dø:ʀ
allein,　was　nützt　der　Kommandör,
but　what　good is　the　commander,

fe:lt⇨　　ɔyç⇨　ɪm　tɔpf　di:　'tsu: bə 'hø:ʀ
fehlt　euch　im　Topf　die　Zubehör?
if are missing　for you　in the　pot　the　ingredients?

kʏm⇨ məl⇨　ɪst　maɪn　'laɪp li: 'kø:ʀ
Kümmel　ist　mein　Leiblikör!
Kümmel　is　my　favorite schnaps!

²) Reflexive pronoun to a verb which is not reflexive in English: sich laben (feast).

TANNHÄUSER
und der Sängerkrieg auf dem Wartburg
music: Richard Wagner
libretto: Richard Wagner (after medieval German history and mythology)

O! du mein holder Abendstern

vi:　'to: dəs 'a: nʊŋ
Wie　Todesahnung,
Like　death's forboding,

'dɛmm rʊŋ　dɛkkt　di:　'lan də
Dämm'rung　deckt　die　Lande;
dusk　veils　the　grounds;

ʊm 'hʏl⇨lt⇨　das　ta:l
umhüllt　das　Tal
covers　the　valley

mɪt　ʃvɛrts lɪ çəm　gə 'van də
mit　schwärzlichem　Gewande.
with (a)　blackish　cloud.

deːᵄ   'zeː lə   diː   nax   'je nən   høːn   fɛʀ 'laŋt
Der   Seele,   die   nach   jenen   Höh'n   verlangt,
The   soul   which   for   those   heights   is longing

foːᵄ   'iː rəm   fluːk   dʊrç   naxt
vor   ihrem   Flug   durch   Nacht
of   its   flight   through   night

ʊnt   'grau zən   baŋt
und   Grausen   bangt.
and   darkness   is afraid.

daː   'ʃaɪ nəst⇨   duː
Da   scheinest   du,
There   shines   you,

oː   'liː⇨ plɪç stɚ   deːᵄ   'ʃtɛr nə
o   lieblichster   der   Sterne;
oh   loveliest   of   stars;

daɪn   'zan⇨ ftəs   lɪçt   ɛnt 'zɛn dəst⇨   duː   deːᵄ   'fɛr nə
dein   sanftes   Licht   entsendest   du   der   Ferne.
your   gentle   light   are sending   you   from   afar.

diː   'nɛːçt gə   'dɛmm rʊŋ
Die   nächt'ge   Dämm'rung
The   nightly   dusk

taɪlt⇨   daɪn   'liː bɚ   ʃtraːl
teilt   dein   lieber   Strahl;
parts   your   dear   ray;

ʊnt   'frɔynt lɪç   tsaɪkst⇨   duː
und   freundlich   zeigst   du
and   friendly   show   you

deːn   veːk   aʊs⇨   deːm   taːl
den   Weg   aus   dem   Tal.
the   way   out of   the   valley.

oː   duː   maɪn   'hɔl dɚ   'aː bɛnt 'ʃtɛrn
O!   du   mein   holder   Abendstern,
Oh!   you   my   beloved   evening star,

voːl   gryːst⇨   ɪç⇨   ɪm⇨ mɚ   dɪç   zoː   gɛrn
wohl   grüßt'   ich   immer   dich   so   gern.
definitely   greeted   I   always   you   so   gladly.

fɔm   'hɛr tsən   das⇨   ziː   niː   fɛʀ 'riːt
Vom   Herzen,   das   sie   nie   verriet,
From the   heart,   which   her   never   betrayed,

'gryː sə   ziː   vɛnn   ziː   foːr 'baɪ   diːᵄ   tsiːt
grüße   sie,   wenn   sie   vorbei   dir   zieht—
greet   her   when   she   by   you   passes—

vɛnn   ziː   ɛnt 'ʃveːpt   deːm   taːl   deːᵄ   'eːr dən
wenn   sie   entschwebt   dem   Tal   der   Erden,
when   she   hovers away   from the   valley   of this   earth

aɪn   zeːl gɚ   'ɛ ŋəl   dɔrt⇨   tsuː   'veːr dən
ein   sel'ger   Engel   dort   zu   werden.
a   blessed   angel   there   to   become.

DIE ZAUBERFLÖTE
music: Wolfgang Amadeus Mozart
libretto: Emanuel Schikaneder (loosely based on a fairytale by Wieland)

Der Vogelfänger bin ich ja

deːᵃ	ˈfoː gəl ˈfɛ ŋɚ	bɪn⇨	⇨nɪç	ja
Der	**Vogelfänger**	**bin**	**ich**	**ja,**
The	*bird catcher*	*am*	*I*	*truly*

ʃteːts	ˈlʊ stɪç	ˈhaɪ sa	ˈhɔp sa sa
stets	**lustig**	**heißa**	**hopsasa!**
always	*jolly*	*yippee*	*hippety hop!*

ɪç	ˈfoː gəl ˈfɛ ŋɚ	bɪn	bə ˈkannt
Ich	**Vogelfänger**	**bin**	**bekannt**
I	*bird catcher*	*am*	*known*

baɪ	alt⇨	ʊnt	jʊŋ	ɪm	ˈgan tsən	lant
bei	**Alt**	**und**	**Jung**	**im**	**ganzen**	**Land.**
by	*old*	*and*	*young*	*in the*	*whole*	*country.*

vaɪs	mɪt⇨	deːm	ˈlɔk⇨ kən	ˈʊm tsuː ˈgeːn
Weiß	**mit**	**dem**	**Locken**	**umzugehn,**
(I) know	*with*	*the*	*bait*	*to deal,*

ʊnt⇨	mɪç	aʊfs	ˈpfaɪ fən	tsuː	fɛʀ ˈʃteːn
und	**mich**	**aufs**	**Pfeifen**	**zu**	**verstehn!**
and	*²)*	*the*	*pipes*	*to*	*skillfully play!*

drʊm	kan⇨	⇨nɪç	froː	ʊnt	ˈlʊ stɪç	zaɪn
Drum	**kann**	**ich**	**froh**	**und**	**lustig**	**sein,**
Therefore	*can*	*I*	*happy*	*and*	*jolly*	*be*

dɛnn	ˈal⇨ lə	ˈføː gəl	zɪnt⇨	jaː	maɪn
denn	**alle**	**Vögel**	**sind**	**ja**	**mein.**
for	*all*	*birds*	*are*	*truly*	*mine.*

aɪn⇨	nɛts	fyːᵃ	ˈmɛː⇨ tçən	ˈmœç tə	ɪç
Ein	**Netz**	**für**	**Mädchen**	**möchte**	**ich;**
A	*net*	*for*	*girls*	*would like*	*I;*

ɪç	fɪŋ	ziː	ˈdʊ⇨ tsɛnt ˈvaɪs	fyːᵃ	mɪç
ich	**fing**	**sie**	**dutzendweis**	**für**	**mich!**
I	*would catch*	*them*	*by the dozen*	*for*	*myself!*

dann	ˈʃpɛr tə	ɪç	ziː	baɪ	miːᵃ	aɪn
Dann	**sperrte**	**ich**	**sie**	**bei**	**mir**	**ein,**
Then	*would lock*	*I*	*them*	*at my place*	*for me*	*up,*

ʊnt	ˈal⇨ lə	ˈmɛː⇨ tçən	ˈvɛː rən	maɪn
und	**alle**	**Mädchen**	**wären**	**mein.**
and	*all*	*girls*	*would be*	*mine.*

vɛnn	'alə lə	'mɛː⇒tçən	wɛː rən	maın
Wenn	**alle**	**Mädchen**	**wären**	**mein,**
If	*all*	*girls*	*would be*	*mine,*

zoː	'tauʃ tə	ıç	braːf	tsʊk⇒ kɚ	aın
so	**tauschte**	**ich**	**brav**	**Zucker**	**ein.**
then	*traded*	*I*	*honestly*	*for sugar.*	¹⁾

diː	'vɛl çə	miːᵃ	am	'liːp⇒ stən	vɛːʀ
Die	**welche**	**mir**	**am**	**liebsten**	**wär',**
The one	*which*	*to me*	*the*	*best*	*would be,*

deːᵃ	gɛː⇒	⇒bıç	glaıç	deːn	'tsʊk⇒ kɚ	heːʀ
der	**gäb'**	**ich**	**gleich**	**den**	**Zucker**	**her.**
to her	*would hand*	*I*	*immediately*	*the*	*sugar*	*over.*

ʊnt	'kʏs⇒ stə	ziː	mıç	'tsɛrt⇒ lıç	dann
Und	**küsste**	**sie**	**mich**	**zärtlich**	**dann,**
And	*kissed*	*she*	*me*	*tenderly*	*then,*

vɛːʀ	ziː	maın	vaıp	ʊnt⇒ ıç	iːᵃ	mann
wär'	**sie**	**mein**	**Weib**	**und ich**	**ihr**	**Mann.**
were	*she*	*my*	*wife*	*and I*	*her*	*husband.*

ziː	ʃliːf	an	maı nɚ	'zaı tə	aın
Sie	**schlief**	**an**	**meiner**	**Seite**	**ein;**
She	*fell asleep*	*at*	*my*	*side;*	¹⁾

ıç	'viːk tə	viː	aın	kın⇒	⇒tsiː	aın
ich	**wiegte**	**wie**	**ein**	**Kind**	**sie**	**ein.**
I	*would rock*	*like*	*a*	*child*	*her*	*to sleep.*

¹⁾ Prefixes to the verbs "eintauschen" (trade, exchange), "einschlafen" (fall asleep)
²⁾ Relative pronoun to the verb "sich verstehen auf ..." (be skillfull in doing something)

Ein Mädchen oder Weibchen

aın	'mɛː⇒ tçən	oː dɚ	'vaı⇒ pçən
Ein	**Mädchen**	**oder**	**Weibchen**
A	*sweetheart*	*or*	*little wife*

vʏnʃt	pa pa 'geː noː	zıç
wünscht	**Papageno**	**sich.**
wishes	*Papageno*	*for himself.*

oː	zoː	aın	'zan⇒ ftəs	'tɔy⇒ pçən
O,	**so**	**ein**	**sanftes**	**Täubchen**
Oh,	*such*	*a*	*tender*	*little dove*

vɛːr	'zeː lıç kaıt	fyːᵃ	mıç
wär'	**Seligkeit**	**für**	**mich.**
would be	*bliss*	*for*	*me.*

dan	'ʃmɛk tə	miːᵃ	'trıŋ kən	ʊnt	ɛs⇒ sən
Dann	**schmeckte**	**mir**	**Trinken**	**und**	**Essen;**
Then	*enjoyed*	*I*	*drinking*	*and*	*eating;*

dan	kœn⇒ tıç	mıt	'fʏr stən	mıç	'mɛs⇒ sən
dann	**könnt'**	**ich**	**mit**	**Fürsten**	**mich**	**messen,**
then	*could*	*I*	*with*	*counts*	*myself*	*rank,*

dɛs	'le: bəns	als	'vaɪ zɚ	mɪç	frɔyn
des	**Lebens**	**als**	**Weiser**	**mich**	**freun,**
(the)	*life*	*as a*	*wise man*	*[2])*	*enjoy,*

ʊnt	vi:	ɪm	e: 'ly: ziʊm	zaɪn
und	**wie**	**im**	**Elysium**	**sein.**
and	*like*	*in (the)*	*Elysium*	*be.*

ax	'kan	⇨nɪç	dɛn	'kaɪ nɚ	fɔn	al⇨ lən
Ach,	**kann**	**ich**	**denn**	**keiner**	**von**	**allen**
Ah,	*can*	*I*	*after all*	*no one*	*of*	*all*

de:n	'raɪ tzən dən	'mɛ:⇨ tçən	gə fal⇨ lən
den	**reizenden**	**Mädchen**	**gefallen?**
the	*charming*	*girls*	*please?*

hɛlf	'aɪ nə	mi:ᵃ	nu:ᵃ	aʊs	de:ᵃ	no:t
Helf'	**eine**	**mir**	**nur**	**aus**	**der**	**Not,**
If helps	*one*	*me*	*only*	*out*	*of (my)*	*need,*

zɔnst	'grɛ:	⇨mɪç	mɪç	'va:r lɪç	tsu:	to:t
sonst	**gräm'**	**ich**	**mich**	**wahrlich**	**zu**	**Tod.**
or else	*will suffer*	*I*	*[2])*	*surely*	*to*	*death.*

vɪrt	'kaɪ nə	mi:ᵃ	'li: bə	gə 'vɛ: rən
Wird	**keine**	**mir**	**Liebe**	**gewähren,**
Will	*no one*	*me*	*love*	*grant,*

zo:	mʊs	mɪç	di:	'flam⇨ mə	fɛʀ 'tse: rən
so	**muss**	**mich**	**die**	**Flamme**	**verzehren;**
or	*must*	*me*	*the*	*flame*	*consume;*

dɔx	kʏst⇨	mɪç⇨	aɪn	vaɪ⇨ plɪçɚ	mʊnt
doch	**küsst**	**mich**	**ein**	**weiblicher**	**Mund,**
but	*if kisses*	*me*	*a*	*female*	*mouth,*

zo:	bɪn⇨	ɪç	ʃo:n	'vi: dɚ	gə 'zʊnt
so	**bin**	**ich**	**schon**	**wieder**	**gesund.**
then	*will be*	*I*	*quickly*	*again*	*well.*

[2]) Reflexive pronouns to the verbs "sich freuen" (enjoy) and "sich grämen" (suffer), which are not reflexive in English. Therefore "sich" is not translated.

THE INTERNATIONAL PHONETIC ALPHABET FOR ENGLISH

An overview of all the sounds found in American Standard (AS),
British Received (RP), and Mid-Atlantic (MA) Pronunciations.
by Kathryn LaBouff

CONSONANTS:

The following symbols are identical to the letters of our English (Roman) Alphabet:

[b], [d], [f], [g], [h], [k], [l], [m], [n], [p], [s], [t], [v], [w], [z]

The symbols below are NEW symbols added because no corresponding symbols exist in the Roman alphabet:

SYMBOL	KEY WORDS
[ŋ]	sing, think
[θ]	thin, thirst
[ð]	thine, this
[ʍ]	whisper, when
[j]	you, yes
[ʃ]	she, sure
[tʃ]	choose, church
[ʒ]	vision, azure
[dʒ]	George, joy
[ɹ]	red, remember, every (the burred r)
[ʀ]	righteousness, great, realm (rolled r)
[r]	very, far away, forever (flip r used between vowels)

VOWELS:

SYMBOL	KEY WORDS
[ɑ]	father, hot ("o" spellings in AS only)
[ɛ]	wed, many, bury
[ɪ]	hit, been, busy
[i]	me, chief, feat, receive
[ɨ]	pretty, lovely
[t]	cat, marry, ask**, charity
[u]	too, wound, blue, juice
[ju]	view, beautiful, usual, tune
[ɯ]	book, bosom, cushion, full
[o]	obey, desolate, melody (unstressed syllables only)
[ɒ]	on, not, honest, God (RP & MA only)*
[ɔ]	awful, call, daughter, sought (AS)
[ɔ̞]	awful, call, daughter, sought (RP & MA)
[ɝ]	learn, burn, rehearse, journey (AS)
[ɜʳ]	learn, burn, rehearse, journey (RP & MA)
[ɚ]	father, doctor, vulgar, elixir (AS)
[əʳ]	father, doctor, vulgar, elixir (RP & MA)
[ʌ]	hum, blood, trouble, judge (stressed syllables)
[ə]	sofa, heaven, nation, joyous (unstressed syllables)

*The use of rolled and flipped R's and the short open o vowel are used in the British RP British and Mid-Atlantic dialect. They should not be used in American Standard dialect.

**[ɝ and ɚ] are the r colored vowels characteristic of American Standard Pronunciation, AS.

[ɜʳ] and [əʳ] are the REDUCED r colored vowels found in British RP, and Mid-Atlantic, MA Pronunciations.

DIPHTHONGS:

SYMBOL	KEY WORDS
[aɪ]	night, buy, sky
[eɪ]	day, break, reign
[ɔɪ]	boy, voice, toil
[oʊ]	no, slow, reproach
[aʊ]	now, about, doubt
[ɛɚ]	air, care, there (AS)
[ɛəʳ]	air, care, there (RP & MA)
[ɪɚ]	ear, dear, here, tier (AS)
[ɪəʳ]	ear, dear, here, tier (RP & MA)
[ɔɚ]	pour, four, soar, o`er (AS)
[ɔəʳ]	pour, four, soar, o`er (RP & MA)
[ʊɚ]	sure, tour, poor (AS)
[ʊəʳ]	sure, tour, poor (RP & MA)
[aɚ]	are, heart, garden (AS)
[aəʳ]	are, heart, garden (RP & MA)

TRIPHTHONGS:

SYMBOL	KEY WORDS
[aɪɚ]	fire, choir, admire (AS)
[aɪəʳ]	fire, choir, admire (RP & MA)
[aʊɚ]	our, flower, tower (AS)
[aʊəʳ]	our, flower, tower (RP & MA)

ADDITIONAL SYMBOLS:

[']   A diacritical mark placed before a syllable that has primary stress.

[ˌ]   A diacritical mark placed before a syllable that has secondary stress.

[ɾ]   A flapped t or d. It is produced by flapping the tongue against the gum ridge. It is very characteristic of medial t's and d's in coloquial and southern American accents.

[ʔ]   A glottalized consonant, usually final or medial t's and d's. It is characteristic of conversational speech patterns in English. Ex: that day- thaʔ day   had done- haʔ done

[(ʊ)]   An off glide symbol. A weak extra vowel sounded after a primary vowel that is characteristic of certain Southern American accents.

GENERAL NOTES:

The texts in this guide have been transcribed into three primary pronunciations: American Standard, British Received and Mid-Atlantic Pronunciations. American Standard is a neutralized pronuncation of American English that is used for the American stage. British Received Pronunciation is an upper class pronunciation that is the performance standard for British works in the United Kingdom. Mid-Atlantic is a hybrid pronunciation that combines elements of both British and North American pronunciation. Some other variants found in this guide are for colloquial American or American Southern accents.

The standard performance practice for these arias was taken into consideration. The transcriptions were based on the character who sings them, the setting of the opera, and the geographic origin of the works. In general, if the composer and/or the text are North American, then the text is transcribed into American Standard pronunciation or one of the American variants. If the composer and or the text are British, then the text is transcribed into British Received Pronunciation. If the composer is North American but the text is British, then the text is transcribed into Mid-Atlantic. These are guidelines. The pronunciations can be modified to accommodate the production values of a specific operatic production or individual artistic taste.

THE BALLAD OF BABY DOE

music: Douglas Moore
libretto: John Latouche (based on the life of Baby Doe Tabor, 1854–1935)

Warm as the autumn light

In American Standard Pronunciation:

wɔɚm æz ði ˈɔtəm laɪt
Warm as the autumn light,

sɔft æz ə pul æʔ naɪt
Soft as a pool at night,

ðə saʊnd əv jɔɚ ˈsɪŋɪŋ
The sound of your singing,

ˈbeɪbɨ doʊ
Baby Doe.

ænd ʍaɪl aɪ wɑz ˈlɪsnɪŋ
And while I was list'ning

aɪ wɑz ɹɪˈkɔlɪŋ
I was recalling

θɪŋz ðæt wʌns aɪ hæd ˈwɑntɪd soʊ mʌtʃ
Things that once I had wanted so much

ænd fɔɚˈgɑtən æz jɪɚz slɪpt əˈweɪ
And forgotten as years slipped away.

ə gɝl aɪ nu bæk hoʊm ɪn vɚˈmɑnt
A girl I knew back home in Vermont

ðə si ɪn nu ˈhæmpʃɚ
The sea in New Hampshire,

ðə fɝst saɪt əv ðə maʊntənz
The first sight of the mountains.

ðeɪ seɪ aɪv bɪn ˈlʌkɨ
They say I've been lucky;

ðɛɚz ˈnʌθɪŋ maɪ ˈmʌnɨ woʊnʔ baɪ
there's nothing my money won't buy.

ɪt ˈkʊdənʔ bi aɪ wɑz ˈʌnˈhæpɨ
It couldn't be I was unhappy

ɔɚ wɑz ˈmɪsɪŋ ðə gʊd θɪŋz əv laɪf
or was missing the good things of life.

bʌt ˈoʊnlɨ tʊˈnaɪt keɪm əˈgɛn ɪn jɔɚ ˈsɪŋɪŋ
But only tonight came again in your singing

ðæt ˈfilɪŋ əv ˈwʌndɚ
That feeling of wonder

əv ˈlɔŋɪŋ ænd peɪn
Of longing and pain.

dip ɪn jɔɚ ˈlʌvlɨ aɪz
Deep in your lovely eyes

ɔl   əv   ɪn'tʃæntmənt   laɪz
All   of   enchantment   lies

ænd   'tɛndɚli   'bɛkənz
And   tenderly   beckons,

'beɪbɨ   dou
Baby   Doe,

'dɹɪɛst   'beɪbɨ   dou
Dearest   Baby   Doe.

VANESSA
music: Samuel Barber
libretto: Gian Carlo Menotti

You rascal, you! I never knew you had a soul
(The Old Doctor's Aria)

In American Standard Pronunciation:

ju   ˈɹæskəl   ju
You   **rascal,**   **you!**

aɪ   ˈnɛvɚ   nju   ju   hæd   ə   soʊl
I   **never**   **knew**   **you**   **had**   **a**   **soul.**

ʌɑt   æn   ˈivnɪŋ
What   **an**   **evening!**

ʌɑt   ˈwɪmɪn   ʌɑt   ˌʃæmˈpeɪn
What   **women,**   **what**   **champagne!**

bʌt   ʌɑt   æm   aɪ   ˈduɪŋ   wɪθ   tu   ˈglæsɪz
But   **what**   **am**   **I**   **doing**   **with**   *two*   **glasses?**

aɪ   mʌst   hæv   bɪn   ˈkæɹɨɪŋ   wʌn   tu   sʌm   ˈtʃɑɚmɪŋ   ˈleɪdɨ
I   **must**   **have**   **been**   **carrying**   **one**   **to**   **some**   **charming**   **lady:**

hu   wɑz   ʃi   oʊ   wɛl
Who   **was**   **she?**   **Oh**   **well...**

aɪ   ʃʊd   ˈnɛvɚ   hæv   bɪn   ə   ˈdɑktɚ   ˈnɪkoləs
I   **should**   **never**   **have**   **been**   **a**   **doctor,**   **Nicholas;**

ə   ˈdʒɛntəlmən   ə   poɛt   ðæts   ʌɑt   aɪ   æm
a   **gentleman,**   **a**   **poet,**   **that's**   **what**   **I**   **am.**

ə   ˈneɪkɪd   ˈbɑdɨ   ʌɑt   ɪz   ɪt   tu   ə   ˈdɑktɚ
A   **naked**   **body,**   **what**   **is**   **it**   **to**   **a**   **doctor?**

wi   si   ðɛm   ˈɛvɹɨ   ˈdeɪ
We   **see**   **them**   **ev'ry**   **day.**

bʌt   ˈʌndɚ   ə   ˌʃændəˈlɪɚ   wɪð   ðə   ɹaɪt   ˈmjuzɪk
But   **under**   **a**   **chandelier,**   **with**   **the**   **right**   **music,**

ðə   ɹaɪt   pɚˈfjum   ə   ˈneɪkɪd   ɑɚm   ə   ˈʃoʊldɚ
the   **right**   **perfume,**   **a**   **naked**   **arm,**   **a**   **shoulder...**

oʊ   gɑd   aɪ   luz   maɪ   maɪnd
Oh   **God,**   **I**   **lose**   **my**   **mind!**

dɪd   ju   si   mi   dæns   wɪð   ˌmamwaˈzɛl   dɔriˈa
Did   **you**   **see**   **me**   **dance**   **with**   **Ma'moiselle**   **Doriat?**

ʃiz   nɑt   soʊ   jʌŋ   aɪ   noʊ   ðæt
She's   **not**   **so**   **young,**   **I**   **know**   **that,**

ə   bɪt   tu   plʌmp   pɚˈhæps
a   **bit**   **too**   **plump,**   **perhaps,**

ə   bɪt   tu   tɔl   fɔɚ   mi
a   **bit**   **too**   **tall**   **for**   **me.**

bʌt   oʊ   soʊ   laɪt   ɑn   hɚ   fit
But,   **oh,**   **so**   **light**   **on**   **her**   **feet,**

souʊ sɔft souʊ blɑnd
so   soft, so   blonde.

dɔkˈtœ dɪə   dɔkˈtœ nɒt kwaɪt souʊ fast dɪə   dɔkˈtœ
"Doctor, dear Doctor, not quite so   fast, dear Doctor!"

hɝ   blu skɑɚf ˈflouʊtɪŋ ˈouʊvɚ maɪ hɛd
Her blue scarf floating over my   head…

hɝ   ˈbuʊzəm ˈhivɪŋ ˈʌndɚ maɪ tʃɪn
her bosom   heaving under my   chin…

u   lɑ lɑ aɪ mʌst stɑp ˈdɹɪŋkɪŋ
Oh la, la! I   must stop drinking.

aɪ stɪl hæv tu əˈnɑuʊns ði ɛnˈgeɪdʒmənt
I   still have to announce the engagement.

jɛs ˈnɪkoləs jɛs ðeɪ tʃouʊz ði ould ˈfæmli ˈdɑktɚ
Yes, Nicholas, yes, they chose the old family doctor

tu   meɪk ði   əˈnɑuʊnsmənt
to   make the announcement.

ə   swit aɪˈdɪə vɛɹi ˈtʌtʃɪŋ
A   sweet idea… very touching.

guʊd ˈhɛvɪnz ʍɛɚ ɪz maɪ spitʃ
Good heavens, where is my   speech?

aɪ ʃuʊd nɑt hæv dɹʌŋk souʊ mʌtʃ
I   should not have drunk so   much;

aɪ ʃæl ˈmʌdəl ʌp ˈɛvɹɨˈθɪŋ
I   shall muddle up   ev'rything.

wɪl ju lɛnd mi jɔɚ kouʊm ˈnɪkoləs
Will you lend me your comb, Nicholas?

ˈvɛɹi ˈtʌtʃɪŋ
Very   touching…